Harvard Business Review

ON

MANAGING THROUGH A DOWNTURN

D1304598

THE HARVARD BUSINESS REVIEW PAPERBACK SERIES

The series is designed to bring today's managers and professionals the fundamental information they need to stay competitive in a fast-moving world. From the preeminent thinkers whose work has defined an entire field to the rising stars who will redefine the way we think about business, here are the leading minds and landmark ideas that have established the *Harvard Business Review* as required reading for ambitious businesspeople in organizations around the globe.

Other books in the series:

Other books in the series (continued):

Harvard Business Review

ON

MANAGING THROUGH A DOWNTURN

The Harvard Business Review articles in this collection are available as individual reprints. Discounts apply to quantity purchases. For information and ordering, please contact Customer Service, Harvard Business School Publishing, Boston, MA 02163. Telephone: (617) 783-7500 or (800) 988-0886, 8 A.M. to 6 P.M. Eastern Time, Monday through Friday. Fax: (617) 783-7555, 24 hours a day. E-mail: custserv@hbsp.harvard.edu.

Library of Congress cataloging information forthcoming
ISBN 978-1-4221-7562-0

Contents

Harvard
Business
Review

ON

MANAGING THROUGH

A DOWNTURN

How Resilience Works

DIANE L. COUTU

Executive Summary

WHY DO SOME PEOPLE BOUNCE BACK from life's hardships while others despair? HBR senior editor Diane Coutu looks at the nature of individual and organizational resilience, issues that have gained special urgency in light of the recent terrorist attacks, war, and recession. In the business arena, resilience has found its way onto the list of qualities sought in employees. As one of Coutu's interviewees puts it, "More than education, more than experience, more than training, a person's level of resilience will determine who succeeds and who fails."

Theories abound about what produces resilience, but three fundamental characteristics seem to set resilient people and companies apart from others. One or two of these qualities make it possible to bounce back from hardship, but true resilience requires all three.

The first characteristic is the capacity to accept and face down reality. In looking hard at reality, we prepare ourselves to act in ways that allow us to endure and survive hardships: We train ourselves how to survive before we ever have to do so.

Second, resilient people and organizations possess an ability to find meaning in some aspects of life. And values are just as important as meaning; value systems at resilient companies change very little over the long haul and are used as scaffolding in times of trouble.

The third building block of resilience is the ability to improvise. Within an arena of personal capabilities or company rules, the ability to solve problems without the usual or obvious tools is a great strength.

WHEN I BEGAN MY CAREER in journalism—I was a reporter at a national magazine in those days—there was a man I'll call Claus Schmidt. He was in his mid-fifties, and to my impressionable eyes, he was the quintessential newsman: cynical at times, but unrelentingly curious and full of life, and often hilariously funny in a sandpaper-dry kind of way. He churned out hard-hitting cover stories and features with a speed and elegance I could only dream of. It always astounded me that he was never promoted to managing editor.

But people who knew Claus better than I did thought of him not just as a great newsman but as a quintessential survivor, someone who had endured in an environment often hostile to talent. He had lived through at least three major changes in the magazine's leadership, losing most of his best friends and colleagues on the way.

At home, two of his children succumbed to incurable illnesses, and a third was killed in a traffic accident. Despite all this—or maybe because of it—he milled around the newsroom day after day, mentoring the cub reporters, talking about the novels he was writing— always looking forward to what the future held for him.

Why do some people suffer real hardships and not falter? Claus Schmidt could have reacted very differently. We've all seen that happen: One person cannot seem to get the confidence back after a layoff; another, persistently depressed, takes a few years off from life after her divorce. The question we would all like answered is, Why? What exactly is that quality of resilience that carries people through life?

It's a question that has fascinated me ever since I first learned of the Holocaust survivors in elementary school. In college, and later in my studies as an affiliate scholar at the Boston Psychoanalytic Society and Institute, I returned to the subject. For the past several months, however, I have looked on it with a new urgency, for it seems to me that the terrorism, war, and recession of recent months have made understanding resilience more important than ever. I have considered both the nature of individual resilience and what makes some organizations as a whole more resilient than others. Why do some people and some companies buckle under pressure? And what makes others bend and ultimately bounce back?

My exploration has taught me much about resilience, although it's a subject none of us will ever understand fully. Indeed, resilience is one of the great puzzles of human nature, like creativity or the religious instinct. But in sifting through psychological research and in reflecting on the many stories of resilience I've heard, I have seen a little more deeply into the hearts and minds of people like Claus Schmidt and, in doing so, looked more deeply into the human psyche as well.

The Buzz About Resilience

Resilience is a hot topic in business these days. Not long ago, I was talking to a senior partner at a respected consulting firm about how to land the very best MBAs—the name of the game in that particular industry. The partner, Daniel Savageau (not his real name), ticked off a long list of qualities his firm sought in its hires: intelligence, ambition, integrity, analytic ability, and so on. "What about resilience?" I asked. "Well, that's very popular right now," he said. "It's the new buzzword. Candidates even tell us they're resilient; they volunteer the information. But frankly, they're just too young to know that about themselves. Resilience is something you realize you have *after* the fact."

"But if you could, would you test for it?" I asked. "Does it matter in business?"

Savageau paused. He's a man in his late forties and a success personally and professionally. Yet it hadn't been a smooth ride to the top. He'd started his life as a poor French Canadian in Woonsocket, Rhode Island, and had lost his father at six. He lucked into a football scholarship but was kicked out of Boston University twice for drinking. He turned his life around in his twenties, married, divorced, remarried, and raised five children. Along the way, he made and lost two fortunes before helping to found the consulting firm he now runs. "Yes, it does matter," he said at last. "In fact, it probably matters more than any of the usual things we look for." In the course of reporting this article, I heard the same assertion time and again. As Dean Becker, the president and CEO of Adaptiv Learning Systems, a four-year-old company in King of Prussia, Pennsylvania, that develops and delivers programs about resilience training, puts it: "More than education, more than experience, more than training, a person's level of resilience will determine who succeeds and who fails. That's true in the cancer ward, it's true in the Olympics, and it's true in the boardroom."

Academic research into resilience started about 40 years ago with pioneering studies by Norman Garmezy, now a professor emeritus at the University of Minnesota in Minneapolis. After studying why many children of schizophrenic parents did not suffer psychological illness as a result of growing up with them, he concluded that a certain quality of resilience played a greater role in mental health than anyone had previously suspected.

Today, theories abound about what makes resilience. Looking at Holocaust victims, Maurice Vanderpol, a former president of the Boston Psychoanalytic Society and Institute, found that many of the healthy survivors of concentration camps had what he calls a "plastic shield." The shield was comprised of several factors, including a sense of humor. Often the humor was black, but nonetheless it provided a critical sense of perspective. Other core characteristics that helped included the ability to form attachments to others and the possession of an inner psychological space that protected the survivors from the intrusions of abusive others. Research about other groups uncovered different qualities associated with resilience. The Search Institute, a Minneapolis-based nonprofit organization that focuses on resilience and youth, found that the more resilient kids have an uncanny ability to get adults to help them out. Still other research showed that resilient inner-city youth often have talents such as athletic abilities that attract others to them.

Many of the early theories about resilience stressed the role of genetics. Some people are just born resilient, so the arguments went. There's some truth to that, of course, but an increasing body of empirical evidence shows that resilience—whether in children, survivors of concentration camps, or businesses back from the brink—can be learned. For example, George Vaillant, the director of the Study of Adult Development at Harvard Medical School in Boston, observes that within various groups studied during a 60-year period, some people became markedly more resilient over their lifetimes. Other psychologists claim that unresilient people more easily develop resiliency skills than those with head starts.

Most of the resilience theories I encountered in my research make good common sense. But I also observed that almost all the theories overlap in three ways. Resilient people, they posit, possess three characteristics: a staunch acceptance of reality; a deep belief, often buttressed by strongly held values, that life is meaningful; and an uncanny ability to improvise. You can bounce back from hardship with just one or two of these qualities, but you will only be truly resilient with all three. These three characteristics hold true for resilient organizations as well. Let's take a look at each of them in turn.

Facing Down Reality

A common belief about resilience is that it stems from an optimistic nature. That's true but only as long as such optimism doesn't distort your sense of reality. In extremely adverse situations, rose-colored thinking can actually spell disaster. This point was made poignantly to me by management researcher and writer Jim Collins, who happened upon this concept while researching *Good to Great,* his book on how companies transform themselves out of mediocrity. Collins had a hunch (an exactly wrong hunch) that resilient companies were filled with optimistic people. He tried out that idea on Admiral Jim Stockdale, who was held prisoner and tortured by the Vietcong for eight years.

Collins recalls: "I asked Stockdale: 'Who didn't make it out of the camps?' And he said, 'Oh, that's easy. It was the optimists. They were the ones who said we were going to be out by Christmas. And then they said we'd be out by Easter and then out by Fourth of July and out by Thanksgiving, and then it was Christmas again.' Then Stockdale turned to me and said, 'You know, I think they all died of broken hearts.'"

In the business world, Collins found the same unblinking attitude shared by executives at all the most successful companies he studied. Like Stockdale, resilient people have very sober and down-to-earth views of those parts of reality that matter for survival. That's not to say that optimism doesn't have its place: In turning around a demoralized sales force, for instance, conjuring a sense of possibility can be a very powerful tool. But for bigger challenges, a cool, almost pessimistic, sense of reality is far more important.

Perhaps you're asking yourself, "Do I truly understand—and accept—the reality of my situation? Does my organization?" Those are good questions, particularly because research suggests most people slip into denial as a coping mechanism. Facing reality, really facing it, is grueling work. Indeed, it can be unpleasant and often emotionally wrenching. Consider the following story of organizational resilience, and see what it means to confront reality.

Prior to September 11, 2001, Morgan Stanley, the famous investment bank, was the largest tenant in the World Trade Center. The company had some 2,700 employees working in the south tower on 22 floors between the 43rd and the 74th. On that horrible day, the first plane hit the north tower at 8:46 AM, and Morgan Stanley started evacuating just one minute later, at 8:47 AM. When the second plane crashed into the south tower 15 minutes after that, Morgan Stanley's offices were largely empty. All told, the company lost only seven employees despite receiving an almost direct hit.

Of course, the organization was just plain lucky to be in the second tower. Cantor Fitzgerald, whose offices were hit in the first attack, couldn't have done anything to save its employees. Still, it was Morgan Stanley's hard-nosed realism that enabled the company to benefit from its luck. Soon after the 1993 attack on the World Trade Center, senior management recognized that working in such a symbolic center of U.S. commercial power made the company vulnerable to attention from terrorists and possible attack.

With this grim realization, Morgan Stanley launched a program of preparedness at the micro level. Few companies take their fire drills seriously. Not so Morgan Stanley, whose VP of security for the Individual Investor Group, Rick Rescorla, brought a military discipline to the job. Rescorla, himself a highly resilient, decorated Vietnam vet, made sure that people were fully drilled about what to do in a catastrophe. When disaster struck on Septem-

ber 11, Rescorla was on a bullhorn telling Morgan Stanley
employees to stay calm and follow their well-practiced
drill, even though some building supervisors were telling
occupants that all was well. Sadly, Rescorla himself,
whose life story has been widely covered in recent
months, was one of the seven who didn't make it out.

"When you're in financial services where so much
depends on technology, contingency planning is a major
part of your business," says President and COO Robert G.
Scott. But Morgan Stanley was prepared for the very
toughest reality. It had not just one, but three, recovery
sites where employees could congregate and business
could take place if work locales were ever disrupted.
"Multiple backup sites seemed like an incredible extrava-
gance on September 10," concedes Scott. "But on September 12, they seemed like genius."

Maybe it was genius; it was undoubtedly resilience at
work. The fact is, when we truly stare down reality, we
prepare ourselves to act in ways that allow us to endure
and survive extraordinary hardship. We train ourselves
how to survive before the fact.

The Search for Meaning

The ability to see reality is closely linked to the second
building block of resilience, the propensity to make
meaning of terrible times. We all know people who,
under duress, throw up their hands and cry, "How can
this be happening to me?" Such people see themselves as
victims, and living through hardship carries no lessons
for them. But resilient people devise constructs about
their suffering to create some sort of meaning for themselves and others.

I have a friend I'll call Jackie Oiseaux who suffered repeated psychoses over a ten-year period due to an undiagnosed bipolar disorder. Today, she holds down a big job in one of the top publishing companies in the country, has a family, and is a prominent member of her church community. When people ask her how she bounced back from her crises, she runs her hands through her hair. "People sometimes say, 'Why me?' But I've always said, 'Why *not* me?' True, I lost many things during my illness," she says, "but I found many more— incredible friends who saw me through the bleakest times and who will give meaning to my life forever."

This dynamic of meaning making is, most researchers agree, the way resilient people build bridges from present-day hardships to a fuller, better constructed future. Those bridges make the present manageable, for lack of a better word, removing the sense that the present is overwhelming. This concept was beautifully articulated by Viktor E. Frankl, an Austrian psychiatrist and an Auschwitz survivor. In the midst of staggering suffering, Frankl invented "meaning therapy," a humanistic therapy technique that helps individuals make the kinds of decisions that will create significance in their lives.

In his book *Man's Search for Meaning*, Frankl described the pivotal moment in the camp when he developed meaning therapy. He was on his way to work one day, worrying whether he should trade his last cigarette for a bowl of soup. He wondered how he was going to work with a new foreman whom he knew to be particularly sadistic. Suddenly, he was disgusted by just how trivial and meaningless his life had become. He realized that to survive, he had to find some purpose. Frankl did so by imagining himself giving a lecture after the war on the psychology of the concentration camp, to help outsiders understand what he had been through. Although he wasn't even sure he would survive, Frankl created some concrete goals for himself. In doing so, he succeeded in rising above the sufferings of the moment. As he put it in his book: "We must never forget that we may also find meaning in life even when confronted with a hopeless situation, when facing a fate that cannot be changed."

Frankl's theory underlies most resilience coaching in business. Indeed, I was struck by how often businesspeople referred to his work. "Resilience training—what we call hardiness—is a way for us to help people construct meaning in their everyday lives," explains Salvatore R. Maddi, a University of California, Irvine psychology professor and the director of the Hardiness Institute in Newport Beach, California. "When people realize the power of resilience training, they often say, 'Doc, is this what psychotherapy is?' But psychotherapy is for people whose lives have fallen apart badly and need repair. We see our work as showing people life skills and attitudes. Maybe those things should be taught at home, maybe they should be taught in schools, but they're not. So we end up doing it in business."

Yet the challenge confronting resilience trainers is often more difficult than we might imagine. Meaning can be elusive, and just because you found it once doesn't mean you'll keep it or find it again. Consider Aleksandr Solzhenitsyn, who survived the war against the Nazis, imprisonment in the gulag, and cancer. Yet when he moved to a farm in peaceful, safe Vermont, he could not cope with the "infantile West." He was unable to discern any real meaning in what he felt to be the destructive and irresponsible freedom of the West. Upset by his critics, he withdrew into his farmhouse, behind a locked fence, seldom to be seen in public. In 1994, a bitter man, Solzhenitsyn moved back to Russia.

Since finding meaning in one's environment is such an important aspect of resilience, it should come as no surprise that the most successful organizations and people possess strong value systems. Strong values infuse an environment with meaning because they offer ways to interpret and shape events. While it's popular these days to ridicule values, it's surely no coincidence that the most resilient organization in the world has been the Catholic Church, which has survived wars, corruption, and schism for more than 2,000 years, thanks largely to its immutable set of values. Businesses that survive also have their creeds, which give them purposes beyond just making money. Strikingly, many companies describe their value systems in religious terms. Pharmaceutical giant Johnson & Johnson, for instance, calls its value system, set out in a document given to every new employee at orientation, the Credo. Parcel company UPS talks constantly about its Noble Purpose.

Value systems at resilient companies change very little over the years and are used as scaffolding in times of trouble. UPS Chairman and CEO Mike Eskew believes that the Noble Purpose helped the company to rally after the agonizing strike in 1997. Says Eskew: "It was a hugely difficult time, like a family feud. Everyone had close friends on both sides of the fence, and it was tough for us to pick sides. But what saved us was our Noble Purpose. Whatever side people were on, they all shared a common set of values. Those values are core to us and never change; they frame most of our important decisions. Our strategy and our mission may change, but our values never do."

The religious connotations of words like "credo," "values," and "noble purpose," however, should not be confused with the actual content of the values. Companies can hold ethically questionable values and still be very resilient. Consider Philip Morris, which has demonstrated impressive resilience in the face of increasing unpopularity. As Jim Collins points out, Philip Morris has very strong values, although we might not agree with them—for instance, the value of "adult choice." But there's no doubt that Philip Morris executives believe strongly in its values, and the strength of their beliefs sets the company apart from most of the other tobacco companies. In this context, it is worth noting that resilience is neither ethically good nor bad. It is merely the skill and the capacity to be robust under conditions of enormous stress and change. As Viktor Frankl wrote: "On the average, only those prisoners could keep alive who, after years of trekking from camp to camp, had lost all scruples in their fight for existence; they were prepared to use every means, honest and otherwise, even brutal . . ., in order to save themselves. We who have come back . . . we know: The best of us did not return."

Values, positive or negative, are actually more important for organizational resilience than having resilient people on the payroll. If resilient employees are all interpreting reality in different ways, their decisions and actions may well conflict, calling into doubt the survival of their organization. And as the weakness of an organization becomes apparent, highly resilient individuals are more likely to jettison the organization than to imperil their own survival.

Ritualized Ingenuity

The third building block of resilience is the ability to make do with whatever is at hand. Psychologists follow the lead of French anthropologist Claude Levi-Strauss in calling this skill bricolage.[1] Intriguingly, the roots of that word are closely tied to the concept of resilience, which literally means "bouncing back." Says Levi-Strauss: "In its old sense, the verb *bricoler . . .* was always used with reference to some extraneous movement: a ball rebounding, a dog straying, or a horse swerving from its direct course to avoid an obstacle."

Bricolage in the modern sense can be defined as a kind of inventiveness, an ability to improvise a solution to a problem without proper or obvious tools or materials. *Bricoleurs* are always tinkering—building radios from household effects or fixing their own cars. They make the most of what they have, putting objects to unfamiliar uses. In the concentration camps, for example, resilient inmates knew to pocket pieces of string or wire whenever they found them. The string or wire might later become useful—to fix a pair of shoes, perhaps, which in freezing conditions might make the difference between life and death.

When situations unravel, bricoleurs muddle through, imagining possibilities where others are confounded. I have two friends, whom I'll call Paul Shields and Mike Andrews, who were roommates throughout their college years. To no one's surprise, when they graduated, they set up a business together, selling educational materials to schools, businesses, and consulting firms. At first, the company was a great success, making both founders paper millionaires. But the recession of the early 1990s hit the company hard, and many core clients fell away. At the same time, Paul experienced a bitter divorce and a depression that made it impossible for him to work. Mike offered to buy Paul out but was instead slapped with a lawsuit claiming that Mike was trying to steal the business. At this point, a less resilient person might have just walked away from the mess. Not Mike. As the case wound through the courts, he kept the company going any way he could—constantly morphing the business until he found a model that worked: going into joint ventures to sell English-language training materials to Russian and Chinese companies. Later, he branched off into publishing newsletters for clients. At one point, he was even writing video scripts for his competitors. Thanks to all this bricolage, by the time the lawsuit was settled in his favor, Mike had an entirely different, and much more solid, business than the one he had started with.

Bricolage can be practiced on a higher level as well. Richard Feynman, winner of the 1965 Nobel Prize in physics, exemplified what I like to think of as intellectual bricolage. Out of pure curiosity, Feynman made himself an expert on cracking safes, not only looking at the mechanics of safecracking but also cobbling together psychological insights about people who used safes and set the locks. He cracked many of the safes at Los Alamos, for instance, because he guessed that theoretical physicists would not set the locks with random code numbers they might forget but would instead use a sequence with mathematical significance. It turned out that the three safes containing all the secrets to the atomic bomb were set to the same mathematical constant, e, whose first six digits are 2.71828.

Resilient organizations are stuffed with bricoleurs, though not all of them, of course, are Richard Feynmans. Indeed, companies that survive regard improvisation as a core skill. Consider UPS, which empowers its drivers to do whatever it takes to deliver packages on time. Says CEO Eskew: "We tell our employees to get the job done. If that means they need to improvise, they improvise.

Otherwise we just couldn't do what we do every day. Just think what can go wrong: a busted traffic light, a flat tire, a bridge washed out. If a snowstorm hits Louisville tonight, a group of people will sit together and discuss how to handle the problem. Nobody tells them to do that. They come together because it's our tradition to do so."

That tradition meant that the company was delivering parcels in southeast Florida just one day after Hurricane Andrew devastated the region in 1992, causing billions of dollars in damage. Many people were living in their cars because their homes had been destroyed, yet UPS drivers and managers sorted packages at a diversion site and made deliveries even to those who were stranded in their cars. It was largely UPS's improvisational skills that enabled it to keep functioning after the catastrophic hit. And the fact that the company continued on gave others a sense of purpose or meaning amid the chaos.

Improvisation of the sort practiced by UPS, however, is a far cry from unbridled creativity. Indeed, much like the military, UPS lives on rules and regulations. As Eskew says: "Drivers always put their keys in the same place. They close the doors the same way. They wear their uniforms the same way. We are a company of precision." He believes that although they may seem stifling, UPS's rules were what allowed the company to bounce back immediately after Hurricane Andrew, for they enabled people to focus on the one or two fixes they needed to make in order to keep going.

Eskew's opinion is echoed by Karl E. Weick, a professor of organizational behavior at the University of Michigan Business School in Ann Arbor and one of the most respected thinkers on organizational psychology. "There is good evidence that when people are put under pressure, they regress to their most habituated ways of responding," Weick has written. "What we do not expect under life-threatening pressure is creativity." In other words, the rules and regulations that make some companies appear less creative may actually make them more resilient in times of real turbulence.

CLAUS SCHMIDT, the newsman I mentioned earlier, died about five years ago, but I'm not sure I could have interviewed him about his own resilience even if he were alive. It would have felt strange, I think, to ask him, "Claus, did you really face down reality? Did you make meaning out of your hardships? Did you improvise your recovery after each professional and personal disaster?" He may not have been able to answer. In my experience, resilient people don't often describe themselves that way. They shrug off their survival stories and very often assign them to luck.

Obviously, luck does have a lot to do with surviving. It was luck that Morgan Stanley was situated in the south tower and could put its preparedness training to work. But being lucky is not the same as being resilient. Resilience is a reflex, a way of facing and understanding the world, that is deeply etched into a person's mind and soul. Resilient people and companies face reality with staunchness, make meaning of hardship instead of crying out in despair, and improvise solutions from thin air. Others do not. This is the nature of resilience, and we will never completely understand it.

Note

1. See, e.g., Karl E. Weick, "The Collapse of Sense-making in Organizations: The Mann Gulch Disaster," *Administrative Science Quarterly*, December 1993.

Originally published in May 2002
Reprint R0205B

Moving Upward in a Downturn

DARRELL RIGBY

Executive Summary

AS THE RECENT BURSTING OF the new economy bubble has shown, business cycles are still with us. The question, then, is, what executives should do to help their companies weather these downturns.

As in so many instances, there are conventional approaches that appear to make sense in the short term. But while these approaches seem reasonable in the heat of the moment, they can eventually damage competitive positions and financial performance.

Drawing on extensive research of *Fortune 500* companies that have lived through industry downturns and economic recessions over the past two decades, Darrell Rigby, a director of Bain & Company, reveals how companies need to go against the grain of convention and exploit industry downturns to harness their unique opportunities for upward mobility.

19

The author explains that every downturn goes through three phases. He examines each phase and shows how successful players navigate the huge waves of a downturn. Smart executives, he says, don't panic: they look bad news in the eye and institutionalize an approach to detecting storms. Rather than hedge their bets through diversification, they focus on their core businesses and spend to gain market share. They manage costs relentlessly during good times and bad. They keep a long-term view and strive to maintain the loyalty of employees, suppliers, and customers. And coming out of the downturn, they maintain momentum in their businesses to stay ahead of the competition they've already surpassed.

Every industry will face periodic downturns of varying severity, says Rigby. But executives with the vision and ingenuity to take unconventional approaches can buoy their companies to new heights.

DOWNTURNS ARE A RECURRING fact of life in every industry. Sooner or later, demand for an industry's products or services declines—often dragging prices down along the way—regardless of the state of the economy as a whole. While it's true that many more industries suffer downturns during recessions, it's a mistake to think that any industry is safe during periods of normal economic growth. In the past two decades, at least 20% of all U.S. industries have battled a downturn in any given year but 1984, when GDP growth soared to more than double the norm.

Given these apparently gloomy facts, what should executives do to help their companies weather a slump? As in so many instances, there are conventional approaches that appear to make sense in the short term. For example, company leaders often approach impending trouble with overconfidence, denying that their industry faces any real danger. Then, when the downturn is an established fact, they make across-the-board cuts of everything from R&D spending to employee head count. Finally, when signs of recovery are everywhere, they turn on the spending spigot to rebuild morale. Although these approaches seem reasonable in the heat of the moment, they can eventually damage competitive positions and financial performance.

Better outcomes are possible, however, if a company's leaders exploit industry downturns to harness their unique opportunities for upward mobility, the same way *Apollo 13*'s astronauts exploited the moon's gravitational pull to escape disaster. Both Arrow Electronics and Emerson (formerly Emerson Electric), for example, followed this path to emerge stronger following downturns. In the late 1980s, financially troubled Arrow launched a series of audacious but intelligent acquisitions during an industry downturn that allowed it to increase sales by more than 500%, turn operating losses into profits, and seize market leadership from a competitor that was once twice its size. Emerson, too, pressed ahead with an investment in a major air-conditioning-processor plant in Thailand during the Asian economic crisis of the late 1990s. While competitors mothballed projects, Emerson ramped up production, exported the plant's products, and secured a strong position for itself in the Asian market when the crisis ended.

To understand how successful companies combat declines in demand, Bain & Company analyzed 377 *Fortune* 500 companies that lived through industry slumps and economic recessions over the last two decades and interviewed nearly 200 of their senior executives. The research found that a downturn evolves through three separate phases. An examination of these phases reveals both the pitfalls that come from following conventional approaches and the rewards that can be reaped by exploiting contrarian opportunities.

Successful players in a downturn place counterintuitive bets in order to dramatically transform their market positions, but these bets are not lucky gambles that miraculously win big against the odds. Instead, they are rigorous and systematic moves that shift the odds in management's favor.

The Gathering Storm

In phase one of a downturn, storm clouds are gathering on the horizon, but industry executives are still basking in memories of sunny years of profitable growth and public accolades. Confidence remains high. As the clouds roll in, however, analysts report that industry growth is slowing, and divisional presidents signal that they might miss their budgets—while still beating the competition, which is doing even worse. Our research found two conventional approaches to such news. Many executives take few if any precautions; they simply act as if the storm will blow over. Others run for cover, investing in new and often unrelated businesses to hedge their bets. But smart executives resist those extremes: they prepare for the worst while focusing their companies on what they do best.

PREPARING FOR THE WORST

As evidence gathers that a downturn is likely, executives often continue to radiate confidence—and even clairvoyance—about the future. They don't want to frighten the troops, which will only make matters worse. Our research shows that most executives are likely to be overly optimistic in the face of an approaching downturn. Some will contend that their industries are safe, period. Others believe that their own company's ability to weather a downturn is superior to that of competitors. As a result of these misguided views, few companies have contingency plans in place that are ready for implementation.

One common concern is that contingency planning will signal a lack of confidence in the company's ability to grow and will thus dampen the organization's morale. Managers also worry that the process will be a waste of time that involves conjuring doomsday scenarios that may never materialize. But these concerns are shortsighted. Failing to plan for the worst is a much bigger mistake than upsetting the troops in the short term, because once an industry is in the middle of a downturn, it is almost impossible for companies to come up with inventive solutions.

Research shows that executives close their minds to new ideas when they are under stress. They tend to reach for the same levers they have pulled in the past, even if those levers don't work in the new conditions. The time to get a range of options out in the open, where they can be broadly and creatively debated, is before a downturn. Managers who are able to successfully negotiate a downturn build contingency planning into the culture of their strategic planning and budgeting processes.

Emerson has been one of the most consistent performers in the *Fortune* 500—it has seen 43 consecutive years of earnings growth—and its performance is the direct result of sophisticated planning systems. Former CEO Charles Knight and his senior managers spent at least half their time planning, and David Farr, who

replaced Knight in the fall of 2000, has continued to
build on Knight's foundation.

At Emerson, each unit must create a monthly report
that reforecasts the remaining quarters of the current
year as well as the first quarter of the next fiscal year. The
monthly reports have been in place for 25 years but are
continually refined. Each report includes a five-column
table that lists growth projections and results. The first
column displays current expected revenue and profits for
the year and by the quarter. The second column shows
expected revenues and profits from the previous month's
report. The third shows the annual budget, and the
fourth indicates actual revenue and profits for the previous year. The fifth column shows the expected percentage increase or decrease over last year's figures. "When I
was a division president, I spent one day a month figur-
ing out what would go into that report," says Farr. "The
whole organization works that way—everyone who provides input to a division head spends one day per month
focused on the future of the business. So if anyone sees a
weakness, a plan to deal with it is immediately created."

Farr combines information from the monthly reports
with that gathered during monthly one-on-one conversations with company business leaders at St. Louis headquarters. Emerson also holds annual planning confer-
ences, during which each division must demonstrate
how it will achieve sales and profit growth, regardless of
conditions in the global economy or the industry. If the
economy slows, Emerson's planning process allows the
company to react quickly to protect sales and profits.
As a result of all this planning, managers know far in
advance of turbulence that if their business environment
changes, they have a well-developed plan to deal with it.
In the late 1990s, Emerson was able to sustain invest-

ment in next-generation process automation—the software and devices that regulate refineries, paper mills, and other industrial plants—while competitors focused on weathering the downturn. So when industry capital spending rebounded, Emerson emerged a stronger player, with sales and profits recovering several quarters ahead of the competition.

FOCUSING ON THE CORE

Here's another piece of conventional wisdom for surviving a downturn: hedge your bets. Pursue growth through diversification. Although this approach works well for individual investors, it makes little sense for corporations.

Contrary to conventional wisdom, downturn winners avoid diversification—and wisely so, because during downturns, typical diversification (the type that enters new businesses with low odds of achieving market leadership) is worse than worthless. It dilutes the company's average market share and therefore subjects it to more earnings volatility, not less. What does make sense is focus, creating ballast by reinforcing the core business. Successful downturn managers avoid diversification and concentrate as many resources as possible on playing to win on their main field of competition.

The example of Borden illustrates the pitfalls of diversification and the wisdom of focusing on core strengths. As the economy started to turn sour in 1980, CEO Eugene Sullivan put Borden, a sprawling $5 billion conglomerate at the time, on a strict diet. He divested the company of high-fat holdings unrelated to the core dairy business, including women's clothing operations, a phosphate rock mine, and a perfume company. Between 1980 and 1985, Sullivan also led the acquisition of 28 companies that were directly related to Borden's core business. As a result of these initiatives, the company's average annual net income was significantly higher than that of competitors throughout this period.

Unfortunately, Sullivan's successor, Romeo Ventres, reversed course: he acquired 90 grocery product companies, which distracted Borden away from its core dairy business. Borden became a jumble of consumer businesses that were spread much too thin across too many lackluster segments, and it was eventually scooped up by RJR Nabisco for $2 billion in stock.

Just as most people on the road assume that they're above-average drivers, most executives feel that their company will do better than competitors when faced with a decline in demand. But without proper planning, that's unlikely. When the weather starts to turn nasty, you can't wait until the last minute to buy batteries and water—by then, the shelves will be empty. Far better to plan ahead and stay focused on what you know you can do, not on what you hope to do better than established players in other markets.

Eye of the Hurricane

At a certain point, questions about an industry downturn become moot. No one can ignore the high winds or copious precipitation falling from the sky. Several smaller competitors are visibly on the brink of ruin. Investor dollars, management talent, and public attention are all seeking higher ground in industries with brighter prospects. Analysts aren't sure how long the downturn will last but express their fears that the industry will never be the same again. Companies think first

Navigating a Downturn

	The conventional approach	The contrarian approach	Success stories
1. Storm clouds on the horizon	Express confidence that *your* industry (or *your* company) is safe from harm.	Build contingency planning into your culture and you'll be prepared for anything.	Emerson, which reforecasts major financial drivers every month.
	Hedge your bets: diversify in the hope that your winners will offset your losers.	Play to win where you are strongest: reinforce your core.	Borden in the early 1980s, which beat competitors by going on a strict corporate diet. (Like so many dieters, Borden put the weight back on in the late 1980s, and its performance suffered.)
2. Battling the elements	Cut costs like there's no tomorrow.	Treat your stakeholders like fellow combatants who happen to be stuck in the same foxhole.	Solectron, which actually increased its focus on quality—its source of competitive advantage—during the recession of the early 1990s.
	On the line in the budget for acquisitions, write "$0."	Scoop up bargains that bolster the core business.	Arrow Electronics, which has followed a "buy in bad times" strategy to become number one in its industry.
3. Here comes the sun	Spend your way back into the good graces of employees and customers.	Don't overstress the engine shift smoothly into higher levels of growth.	Emerson, which handled phases one and two deftly during the recession of the early 1990s, steadily added people, R&D dollars, and capacity to maintain growth.
			American Express, meanwhile, stumbled badly during the early 1990s. But it used the more forgiving post-recession climate to completely retool its business.

and foremost about survival. Conventional wisdom urges quick and drastic action and cautions against acquisitions spending. Clearly, this is a time when costs must be reined in—but prudently. Smart companies look beyond the storm and even find ways to grow while it rages around them.

SEEING BEYOND THE BAD TIMES

When an industry's news is universally bad, managers tend to want to apply quick fixes. To cut costs quickly and spread the pain as fairly as possible, they slash budgets and staff across the board. They slice sales and earnings targets. They also reduce capital expenditures, drop services that competitors don't offer, and push suppliers to cut prices. In other words, their focus becomes short-term survival.

This is not unreasonable. Aggressive cost management is extremely important during a downturn, just as it is during an upturn. The problem is, many executives overreact to disturbing economic reports. Layoffs, for example, are often implemented as a way of holding down costs, but do they really make financial sense? Consider that voluntary employee turnover averages 15% to 20% per year in the United States, that sales volume was depressed by less than 10% in 85% of all industry downturns from 1977 to 1999, and that the average recession during that period lasted only 11 months. Given those facts, you have to wonder why there is such a scramble to fire—and then rehire and retrain—so many employees.

Squeezing suppliers is another short-term fix that can do more harm than good. Consider the tale of two Chryslers. During the recession of 1990 and 1991, Chrysler's approach was brilliant. Rather than forcing suppliers to share the pain, the company developed closer relations with them, outsourcing more components, reducing inventory, and slashing cycle times. If suppliers suggested ways to cut costs by 10%, they got half the savings. Chrysler used improved cash flows to invest in new product development, introducing cross-functional platform teams to improve quality and speed. Partly as a result of its work with suppliers—as well as judicious cost cutting—Chrysler was the only Big Three automaker to turn a profit in 1992.

Over time, Chrysler's hard-won cost advantage slipped, and now a different story appears to be in the making. The cornerstone of the current turnaround attempts is a supplier squeeze. Since January 1, 2001, all suppliers have been required to tear up existing contracts, reduce prices by 5%, and figure out how to cut an additional 10% from prices by 2003. Some suppliers are suggesting that they may withhold parts, and others have said they no longer have any incentive to bring Chrysler their best technologies. As a result of its tough stance, Chrysler may end up paying much more than it saves.

Costs do have to be carefully managed, but the key is consistency. A company shouldn't act one way in good times and another way in bad times. Otherwise, employees, suppliers, and other business partners will lose confidence in the company, and morale, cooperation, and productivity will all decline.

Now look to the contrarians. They know that downturns don't last forever and, in effect, they make friends with others who are trapped in the same foxhole—employees, vendors, business partners, and customers. They know that forcing a relatively small price cut (which will be remembered when the tables are turned) on suppliers is typically far less valuable than working with them to eliminate duplicate operations, improve forecasts, reduce inventories, and improve cycle times. They understand that although employee layoffs will reduce costs in the short term, the combination of severance expenses, loss of knowledge and trust, and subsequent hiring, training, and retention costs can quickly overwhelm expected savings. Companies such as Southwest Airlines, Harley-Davidson, and FedEx have no-layoff policies. As a result, their employees dig in during tough times rather than shop for new jobs.

Some companies have used downturns to build loyalty with other stakeholders. For example, electronic components manufacturer Solectron used the recession of the early 1990s to build customer loyalty. It did so by maintaining an unwavering focus on quality, the driving force behind its ability to attract and retain such customers as IBM, Hewlett-Packard, and Sun Microsystems. When demand fell in 1991, it increased its focus on quality and customer retention by interviewing customers weekly to check satisfaction. The company also added low-cost capacity in Malaysia that year to gain market share. These efforts during a downturn paid off handsomely: in 1991, Solectron won a Baldrige Quality Award, increased revenues by more than 50%, and replaced SCI Systems as the market leader. By focusing on the long term, Solectron has outperformed its competitors for more than a decade. Even as the industry slumps again this year, analysts predict that the company will grow 70% faster than SCI Systems between 2000 and 2002.

SHOPPING FOR BARGAINS

Conventional wisdom says that acquisitions are too risky to undertake during a downturn. According to this way of thinking, companies that appear ripe for the picking are likely to be deeply troubled and could drag down an already fragile business. Moreover, a company thinking about acquisitions may find that its cash is limited, that debt is unavailable, and that its stock price is depressed and thus not valuable as acquisition currency. Given these dismal conditions, the last thing a company should do is double down existing bets with acquisitions.

In keeping with this logic, only 20% of executives in our survey said they would be likely to make acquisitions during a future downturn, while 50% said they would be unlikely to do so (the rest were undecided). But clear winners in a downturn don't lock their purses; they spend on bargains, as the following example demonstrates.

In May 1985, the electronic components industry had hit a wall. It marked the beginning of a three-year slump that nearly drove Arrow Electronics into the ground. "We had $30 million worth of interest due that year and no operating income," CEO Steve Kaufman tells us. "We were losing big chunks of cash." Sales were collapsing, dropping from $730 million in 1984 to $550 million in 1987. Kaufman had already disposed of the company's sideline businesses in lead smelting and electrical distribution. Although Arrow was number two in the industry, it was about half the size of the leader in the field.

Rather than cut back in the hope of surviving, Kaufman took advantage of the turbulence. "We made our greatest strategic moves during the period of greatest financial weakness," he says. He decided to get out of the hole through acquisitions. In 1987, Arrow bought the number three player. It funded the purchase with one-third Arrow stock and two-thirds cash that was borrowed against the acquisition target's receivables and inventory. One competitor snickered that the deal looked "like two men who can't swim grabbing each other in the deep end of the pool." But it worked. In the first full year after the acquisition, Arrow registered a modest net profit of $10 million. In 1991, Kaufman bought the new number three company, which was suffering during what turned out to be a little blip of an industry downturn. The deal was an exact replica of the 1987 acquisition. After several more acquisitions in Europe, Arrow swept past Avnet, the industry leader, to take the top position in the field. Kaufman looks upon the inevitable downturns in the electronic components business as an opportunity: "We acquire in bad times," he says. The surprising insight is that—assuming the core business is worth holding and growing—focused acquisitions during downturns should reduce risk, not increase it. As the Arrow example demonstrates, consolidating acquisitions diminishes business risk by strengthening the core and reducing earnings volatility.

Clear Skies on the Horizon

In the final phase of a downturn, portents of economic renewal emerge. Industry analysts begin to predict a turnaround, although they may be vague about the timing. Competitors start to take advantage of lowered interest rates to expand capacity and boost inventories in anticipation of rising sales. New orders start to flow in, and hitting next year's budget figures seems realistic. Conventional wisdom says that companies should make an abrupt about-face and shift into high-spending mode. But again, this is flawed advice. Companies that have successfully managed the first two phases of a downturn won't need to put the pedal to the floor. Those that remain beleaguered should consider completely overhauling the way they do business.

ACCELERATING SMOOTHLY

Preparing to exit a downturn is either the easiest or the hardest stage of management. Companies that properly managed the first two phases of a downturn seldom need much advice in the third. They have mapped out and implemented contingency plans to deftly sidestep unexpected hazards. They have pruned share-diluting businesses and strengthened their core. They have bolstered vital relationships with employees, vendors, business partners, and customers. They have made share-boosting acquisitions at attractive prices. As a result of these moves, they have captured a disproportionate share of industry growth and profits. Now they are prepared to accelerate gradually and reap the rewards.

As the recession of 1990 and 1991 wound down, Emerson smoothly ramped up from a sales decline of 2% in 1991 to growth rates of 4% in 1992 and on to 16% by 1995. CEO Knight has steadily added people, R&D dollars, and capacity to maintain the company's return on assets at between 9% and 11% every year since 1990.

But Emerson's success is uncommon. In fact, more businesses fail after a downturn than during one. Part of the reason is that it takes a while for downturn-diseased companies to die. But a bigger part of the reason is that actions taken during the exit phase are inadequate to position the company for renewed growth.

COMPLETELY RETOOLING

After a painful time, executives often hope they can mend the damage by flipping on the spending switch. Their rationale is simple: since draconian cuts have seriously damaged the loyalty and morale of beleaguered employees, generous spending is now essential to regain their affections. In addition, heavy marketing, promotion, and service investments are needed to win back customers who defected when they grew exasperated with quality reductions and service cutbacks. Unfortunately, as companies in the motor vehicle and oil and gas industries have discovered, spending increases in this situation often outpace growth, forcing companies to make drastic cuts again when the next downturn hits.

Companies that fell behind in the first two phases require serious rehabilitation in this last phase if they hope to survive another downturn. Rather than try to spend their way out of their misery, troubled companies should consider retooling altogether. Such retooling may require a mix of the approaches outlined earlier but on a greater scale, from jettisoning noncore businesses to slashing costs. The difference is the warmer business climate: as industry conditions improve for what could be several years of growth, down-and-out companies have a better chance of successfully reinventing themselves.

American Express followed this path after emerging from the recession of the early 1990s in very poor shape. Strong new competition had led to a 1.6 million decline in the number of AmEx cards in circulation, and those who kept their cards were using them less and less. In 1991, about 100 restaurants in Boston threatened to boycott AmEx in protest over unreasonable transaction fees. Compounding these problems, the company had to write off $265 million in bad loans made to customers of American Express's credit card offering, Optima.

In 1993, the AmEx board ousted chief executive James D. Robinson III. Robinson's successor, Harvey Golub, set about rehabilitating and reshaping the company to take advantage of the expected upswing in consumer spending and prepare it for future slowdowns. He began by divesting noncore businesses like Shearson, a brokerage firm. Then he attacked costs, seeing the advantage of making the company lean in good economic times. By 1994, he had cut $3 billion in costs, along with 15,800 jobs. Although such pruning was painful, it prepared the company to grow as it recovered from the troubles of the early 1990s. If such drastic measures had been taken during a downturn, they would have hampered the company's ability to return to profitability. They might have destroyed the confidence of AmEx's organization and shareholders, eventually requiring even more dramatic actions and leading the company on a downward spiral.

Golub's third campaign was to refocus AmEx on its core business—charge and credit cards. For example, he successfully challenged the elitist attitude in the company that opposed allowing customers to use AmEx cards at gas stations. He also broadened the pool of retailing partners, signing up Kmart in 1993 and Wal-Mart in 1995.

As a result of these forceful measures, the company came back strong during good economic times. In 1994, the number of cards in circulation began to increase, rising from about 25 million to more than 29 million by 1996. The company introduced many new products, building its market share from 17% in 1994 to almost 21% in 1998. Its stock outperformed the S&P index by three-and-a-half times between December 1991 and the end of the decade.

As the story of American Express demonstrates, failure to strengthen the company during a downturn can leave it in a much tougher position afterward. At that point, dramatic changes will likely be required. The company may need to refocus on its core, prune its portfolio, and bring in new management, not only to bring fresh

energy and breakthrough perspectives, but also to convince key stakeholders (especially employees) that the
reinvention is for real. The new team needs to establish a
core set of values and make it clear that the company
will adhere to them in good times and in bad. To avoid
wild spending swings, it has to establish cost structures
that can be sustained through a downturn.

And then, after several years of profitable growth and
public accolades for the management team, economic
storm clouds will enter the scene . . . again. But the
company will be much better positioned this time to
handle the bad weather.

Look to the Lighthouse

Making it through the three phases of a downturn isn't
easy, and there's no guaranteed path to success. Nevertheless, our research findings may provide a beam of
light to help companies see their way through a storm.
Companies that successfully navigate huge waves tend
to look bad news in the eye and institutionalize an
approach to detecting storms. Rather than hedge their
bets through diversification, they place a big bet on their
core businesses and spend to gain market share. They
manage costs relentlessly during good times and bad.
They maintain a long-term view and strive to earn the
loyalty of employees, suppliers, and customers. Coming
out of the downturn, they maintain momentum in their
businesses to stay ahead of the competition they've
already surpassed.

As the recent bursting of the dot-com bubble has
shown, business is still subject to cyclical change. Every
industry will face periodic downturns of varying severity.

Executives with the vision, ingenuity, and courage to go against the grain of convention can buoy their companies to new heights while competitors are sinking.

Originally published in June 2001
Reprint R0106F

When Growth Stalls

MATTHEW S. OLSON, DEREK VAN BEVER, AND
SETH VERRY

Executive Summary

AN ABRUPT AND LASTING DROP in revenue growth is
a crisis that can strike even the most exemplary organization. The authors' comprehensive analysis of growth in
Fortune 100-size companies over the past half century
revealed, in fact, that 87% of them had stalled out at
least once. The record shows that if management cannot
turn a company around within a few years, the odds are
that it will never again see healthy top-line growth.

Fortunately, Olson, van Bever, and Verry, of the Corporate Executive Board, have uncovered and catego-
rized the most common causes of growth stalls. The majority of these standstills are preventable because, according
to the authors, they arise from management choices about
strategy or organizational design; external factors, such
as regulatory actions or economic downturns, account for
only 13%. Four categories predominate:

Premium-position captivity. When a firm's world-class offering has won the most demanding customers in the market, it often fails to respond effectively to new, low-cost competitive challenges or shifts in customer valuation of product features.

Innovation management breakdown. Because most large corporations generate sequential product innovations, any systemic inefficiency or dysfunction in the innovation chain can cause extremely serious problems that last for years.

Premature core abandonment. Managers may conclude too quickly that a core market is saturated. Or they may incorrectly interpret operational impediments in the core business as evidence that it's time to move into new competitive terrain.

Talent bench shortfall. Insufficient capabilities—particularly at the executive level and typically in areas of acute and specialized need—will stop growth dead in its tracks.

The authors also identified a common culprit in detailed case studies of 50 stalled companies—failure to adapt the assumptions that drive company strategy to changes in the external environment. Two tools can help managers avoid growth stalls: a self-test to diagnose impending stalls and a choice of practices to explicitly identify strategic assumptions and test them for ongoing relevance.

Senior management at Levi Strauss & Company could be forgiven for not seeing it coming. The year was 1996. The company had just achieved a personal best, with sales cresting $7 billion for the first time in its history. This performance extended a run of growth in which overall revenue had more than doubled within a decade. Since taking the company private in 1985, management had relaunched the flagship 501 brand, introduced the Dockers line of khaki pants, and increased international sales from 23% to 38% of revenue and more than 50% of profits. Growth in 1995 was the strongest it had been in recent years.

And then came the stall. From that high-water mark of 1996, company sales went into free fall. Year-end revenue results for 2000 were $4.6 billion—a 35% decline from four years prior. Market value declined even more precipitously: Analysts estimate that it went from $14 billion to $8 billion in those four years. The company's share of its core U.S. jeans market dropped by half over the 1990s, falling from 31% in 1990 to 14% by decade's end. Today, with a new management team in place, Levi Strauss has undergone a company-wide transformation. It may be regaining its footing, but it has yet to return to growth.

While more dramatic than many, this is the story of a revenue growth stall—a crisis that can hit even the most exemplary organizations. It shares many elements with other stalls, at companies as varied as 3M, Apple, Banc One, Caterpillar, Daimler-Benz, Toys "R" Us, and Volvo. What these companies would surely recognize in the story is the stall's suddenness. Like Levi Strauss, most organizations actually accelerate into a stall, experiencing unprecedented progress along key measures just before growth rates tumble. When the momentum is lost, it's as if the props have been knocked out from under their corporate strategy. (See the exhibit "No Soft Landings.") Typically, few on the senior team see the stall coming; core performance metrics often fail to register trouble on the horizon.

No Soft Landings

An analysis of the growth histories of Fortune 100 and Global 100 companies that experienced stalls between 1955 and 2006 reveals this composite pattern. After a burst of energy, growth does not descend gradually; it drops like a stone.

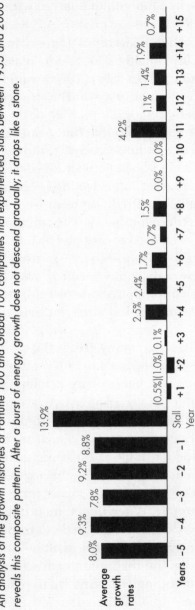

As part of our ongoing research into growth, the Corporate Executive Board recently completed a comprehensive analysis of the growth experiences of some 500 leading corporations in the past half century, focusing particularly on "stall points"—our term for the start of secular reversals in company growth fortunes, as opposed to quarterly stumbles or temporary corrections. The companies in our study included more than 400 that have appeared on the *Fortune* 100 since that index was created, some 50 years ago, along with about 90 non-U.S. companies of a similar size. The study revealed patterns in the incidence, costs, and root causes of growth stalls. (Our research approach is described briefly in "The Search for Stall Points" at the end of this article.)

On the quantitative record alone, we can attest that Levi Strauss is in good company: 87% of the companies in this group have suffered one or more stall points. We can also appreciate the consequences of such events. On average, companies lose 74% of their market capitalization, as measured against the S&P 500 index, in the decade surrounding a growth stall. More often than not, the CEO and senior team are replaced in its aftermath. And unless management is able to diagnose the causes of a stall and get the company back on track quickly—turning it around in a matter of several years—the odds are against its ever returning to healthy top-line growth.

Deeper analysis sheds light on the most common causes of growth stalls, which turn out to be preventable for the most part. There is a common assumption that when the fortunes of great companies plunge, it must be owing to big, external forces—economic meltdowns, acts of God, or government rulings—for which management cannot be held accountable. In fact most stalls occur for reasons that are both knowable and addressable at the time. The exhibit "The Root Causes of Revenue Stalls" reveals the factors that lay behind the stalls of 50 companies we went on to study in depth; clearly, a company can falter in many ways. One might almost think that sustaining growth in a very large company depends on doing absolutely everything right. But the root causes of stalls are not so varied or complex that we can't see patterns.

What the exhibit demonstrates is that the vast majority of stall factors result from a choice about strategy or organizational design. They are, in other words, controllable by management. Further, even within this broad realm, nearly half of all root causes fall into one of four categories: premium-position captivity, innovation management breakdown, premature core abandonment, and talent bench shortfall.

In this article we'll offer advice for avoiding these hazards, drawing from practices currently in use at large, high-growth companies to foresee possible stalls and head them off. More generally we will explore why management is so often blindsided by these events. As we will show, a large number of global companies may at this moment be perilously close to their own stall points. Knowing how to avoid growth stalls begins with understanding their causes. Let's look at each of the four categories.

When a Premium Position Backfires

By far the largest category of factors responsible for serious revenue stalls is what we have labeled premium-position captivity: the inability of a firm to respond effectively to new, low-cost competitive challenges or to a significant shift in customer valuation of product features.

We use the term "captivity" because it suggests how management teams can be hemmed in by a long history of success. A company that solidly occupies a premium market position remains insulated longer than its competitors against evolution in the external environment. It has less reason to doubt its business model, which has historically provided a competitive advantage, and once it perceives the crisis, it changes too little too late. When the towering strengths of a firm are transformed into towering weaknesses, it's a cruel reversal.

Readers will recognize the intellectual kinship between our notion of premium-position captivity and the patterns of technology disruption described by Clayton M. Christensen in his landmark book *The Innovator's Dilemma* (Harvard Business School Press, 1997). As we scan the broad data set of the *Fortune* 100 over the past half century, we are struck by Christensen's acumen. In documenting premium-position captivity in leading enterprises, we saw a cycle of disdain, denial, and rationalization that kept many management teams from responding meaningfully to market changes.

Price and quality leaders such as Eastman Kodak and Caterpillar, for example, have found themselves unable (or unwilling) to formulate a timely, effective response to the threat posed by foreign entrants. The owners of iconic brands, such as American Express, Heinz, and Procter & Gamble, may assume that the decades-long investments they have made in their brands will protect their premium prices against lower-cost entrants. Both Compaq and Philip Morris (now part of Altria) failed to respond to signs of trouble in the early 1990s because they relied on performance metrics designed around generous margins.

We saw premium-position captivity at work in the Levi Strauss stall when the company failed to spot a strategic inflection in customer demand. In cases like this one, organizations and their multiple sophisticated

The Root Causes of Revenue Stalls

A careful analysis of 50 representative companies that experienced growth stalls revealed nearly as many root causes for them: 42 external, strategic, and organizational factors, which can be grouped into categories as shown here. We identified the top three factors contributing to each company's stall and considered those results as a whole in determining how large a role (indicated by percentage) each category played. The clustering that is at the heart of our findings is clear: Four categories account for more than half the occurrences of root causes we cataloged—premium-position captivity, innovation management break-down, premature core abandonment, and talent bench shortfall.

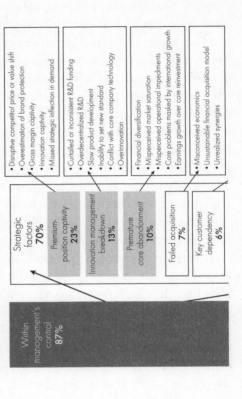

Within management's control
87%

Strategic factors
70%

Premium-position captivity
23%
- Disruptive competitor price or value shift
- Overestimation of brand protection
- Gross margin captivity
- Innovation captivity
- Missed strategic inflection in demand

Innovation management breakdown
13%
- Curtailed or inconsistent R&D funding
- Overdecentralized R&D
- Slow product development
- Inability to set new standard
- Conflict with core company technology
- Overinnovation

Premature core abandonment
10%
- Financial diversification
- Misperceived market saturation
- Misperceived operational impediments
- Core problems masked by international growth
- Earnings growth over core reinvestment

Failed acquisition
7%
- Misconceived economics
- Unsustainable financial acquisition model
- Unrealized synergies

Key customer dependency
6%

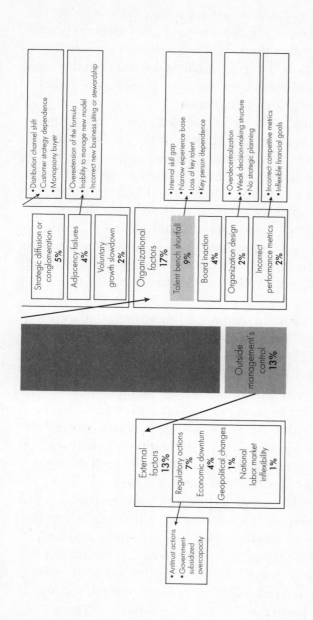

External factors
13%

Regulatory actions **7%**
Economic downturn **4%**
Geopolitical changes **1%**
National labor market inflexibility **1%**

- Antitrust actions
- Government-subsidized overcapacity

Outside management's control **13%**

Strategic diffusion or conglomeration **5%**

- Distribution channel shift
- Customer strategy dependence
- Monopsony buyer

Adjacency failures **4%**

- Overextension of the formula
- Inability to manage new model
- Incorrect new business siting or stewardship

Voluntary growth slowdown **2%**

Organizational factors **17%**

Talent bench shortfall **9%**

- Internal skill gap
- Narrow experience base
- Loss of key talent
- Key person dependence

Board inaction **4%**

Organization design **2%**

- Overdecentralization
- Weak decision-making structure
- No strategic planning

Incorrect performance metrics **2%**

- Incorrect competitive metrics
- Inflexible financial goals

market-sensing activities simply don't recognize the importance of an emerging behavior or customer preference in their core markets. They continue to place their bets on product or service attributes that are in decline, while disruptive entrants emphasizing different, under-recognized features gain ground.

In the early 1990s Levi Strauss enjoyed surging revenues even as its relationships with the Gap and other distributors faltered and as designers and retailers introduced jeans products at the high and low ends of the market. The rise of house brands and superpremium designer jeans looked manageable—or ignorable—as long as healthy revenue growth continued. By the time the growth stall had become evident, the company found itself with an expensive retailing strategy and a product line that was out of step with both ends of the denim jeans market.

The market data relating to this growth stall were not hidden from Levi Strauss executives; the challenge was to separate the signal from the noise. The company's years of success warped its interpretation of what it was seeing. Its story illustrates how difficult it is to respond to a threat in the absence of a burning platform: If your sales are continuing to rise, how do you focus concern? In 1999 Gordon Shank, then the company's chief marketing officer, admitted ruefully, "We didn't read the signs that all was not well. Or we were in denial."

Although the onset of premium-position captivity is gradual, there are often clues that trouble is afoot, both in the external market and in executive attitudes and behaviors. (See the sidebar "When Does a Premium Position Become a Trap?" at the end of this article.) Easiest to spot in marketing data are pockets of rapid market share loss, particularly in narrow customer segments, and increasing resistance among key customers to solutions wrappers and other bundling of services. It can also be revealing to focus on metrics different from those you ordinarily emphasize. If you normally track profit per customer, for example, you are content when it rises. But would you notice if customer acquisition costs increased even more rapidly? When it comes to management attitudes, your ears may pick up the strongest clues: Listen closely to the tone in the executive suite when conversation turns to upstart competitors or to successful rivals that are viewed as less capable. Is it acceptable, or routine, to dismiss them as unworthy? Do your processes for gathering intelligence about your competitors ignore some of these market participants because of their size or perceived lack of quality? Indulging in such behavior is common, but it's a luxury that no market leader can afford.

When Innovation Management Breaks Down

The second most frequent cause of growth stalls is what we call innovation management breakdown: some chronic problem in managing the internal business processes for updating existing products and services and creating new ones. We saw manifestations of this at every major stage along the activity chain of product innovation, from basic research and development to product commercialization.

Where revenue growth stalls could be attributed to innovation breakdown, the problems emphatically did not center on individual product launch failures; a New Coke may occasionally belly flop, but the result is typically a temporary growth stumble rather than a fateful turning point in a company's growth history. By contrast, the secular growth stalls we identified were attributable to systemic inefficiencies or dysfunctions. Given that most large corporations rely on business models that have evolved to generate sequential product innovations, when things go wrong here—at the heart of these organizations' most important business process—extremely serious, multiyear problems result.

For firms shifting the bulk of their R&D activities out to their business units, our case studies provide a strong cautionary tale. The logic behind such shifts is clear: The closer R&D is to markets and individual unit strategies, the higher its return on investment should be. But problems seem to arise when decentralization is combined with an explicit (or implicit) metric that demands a high share of revenue growth from new-product introductions. The result can be an overallocation of resources to ever smaller incremental product opportunities, at the expense of sustained R&D investment in larger, future product platforms.

A stark example of this occurred at 3M in the 1970s, when the company experienced a revenue stall after decades of robust top-line growth. Since its founding, in 1902, 3M had followed a clear formula for success, developing innovative products with industrial applications that supported a premium position and then leapfrogging to the next opportunity as the market matured. This strategy, which has been characterized as "the corporate millipede" ("Make a little, sell a little, make a little more"), had by the early 1970s produced a portfolio of more than 60,000 products (the majority of them with sales under $100 million), while more than 25% of total corporate sales came from products less than five years old.

The growth potential inherent in this niche-jumping strategy began to dwindle in the late 1970s, as the firm approached $5 billion in revenue. With the recession of the early 1980s looming, 3M management decided to hold R&D expenditures below historical averages of just over 6% of annual sales and to push most of the R&D budget down to the company's 42 divisions (usually organized around individual product lines).

Total growth slowed as divisions focused on ever narrower niche-segment opportunities. From 1979 to 1982 the company saw its annual growth rate fall from 17% to just over 1%, with sales per employee creeping downward simultaneously. Because the bulk of R&D was controlled by product-centric business units, major new-product development activity was replaced by incremental product line extensions. The former CEO Allen F. Jacobson observed of that era, "Historically, our drive for profit and our preference for developing premium-priced products aimed at market niches meant that we were not comfortable competing only on price. As a result, we never fully developed our manufacturing competencies. And when competitors followed us, we would refuse to confront them—it was always easier to innovate our way into a new niche."

As we looked at the variety of ways in which problems in the innovation management process can eventually produce major revenue stalls, we were struck by the fragility of this chain of activities, and by how vulnerable the whole process is to management decisions made to achieve perfectly valid corporate goals. There are some powerful clues, however, when a company is at serious risk. Most significant is probably not the overall level of R&D spending but how those dollars are being spent. Is the senior team able to look into

funding decisions at the business unit level to monitor
the balance between incremental and next-generation
investments? Are R&D and other innovation resources
at the corporate level budgeted separately from incremental innovation? Is some portion of innovation
funding allocated to creating lower-cost versions of
existing products and services? Given the long lead
times characteristic of the innovation process, flaws
are slow to surface—and time-consuming to remedy.

When a Core Business Is Abandoned

The third major cause of revenue stalls is premature core
abandonment: the failure to fully exploit growth opportunities in the existing core business. Its telltale markers
are acquisitions or growth initiatives in areas relatively
distant from existing customers, products, and channels.

   This category has received significant attention in the
recent business literature. Perhaps as a result, stalls
attributed to premature core abandonment cluster in the
period before 1990. We are tempted to credit the management consulting industry for having hammered home
the need for attention to core businesses. In particular,
Chris Zook, of Bain & Company, has stayed on this issue
with ferocity.

   That is not to say that *Fortune* 100–size firms have
mastered the art of generating continuous growth in
their core businesses. Quite the contrary: The recent
wave of private equity takeovers suggests that many
public companies still struggle in their efforts to grow
established businesses. Almost without exception, these
take-overs are based on strategies for growing the core—
strategies that public-company executive teams are
either unable or unwilling to pursue.

The two most common mistakes we saw in this category were believing that one's core markets are saturated and viewing operational impediments in the core business model as a signal to move on to new, presumably easier competitive terrain. Either situation invariably ended badly, with some competitor moving in to displace the incumbent.

In the late 1960s Robert Sarnoff, the CEO of RCA and son of David Sarnoff, the legendary force behind the company, came to the mistaken belief that "the age of the big breakthroughs in consumer electronics—the age in which [his father] had built RCA—had passed." James Hillier, the head of the company's labs, asserted, "The physicists have discovered about all they are going to for consumer application in the near future."

One can hardly blame Sarnoff when even the physicists were advocating moving on—and move on he did. He pursued initiatives in three new, presumably higher-growth directions. First, mainframe computers seemed a logical choice, given that technology-driven big bets had powered RCA's growth since the 1920s. Second, he decided that marketing was the future and deployed huge resources to acquire companies in the consumer products sector. Third, the company redirected internal resources from consumer electronics research into marketing and brand management projects. Meanwhile, Steve Jobs and Bill Gates were on the road to starting companies that would launch a revolution in RCA's former core markets.

Just as interesting as getting it wrong on core business growth prospects is the tendency of executive teams to simply give up on apparently intractable problems in their core businesses. The most intriguing example of this occurred at Kmart. A highly successful challenger to

Sears as a general-merchandise big-box retailer, Kmart relentlessly stole its formerly indomitable competitor's market share through the 1960s and 1970s.

In 1976 Kmart reached a peak in new store openings, adding 271 facilities to its countrywide network. That would prove to be its limit. Over the next decade the company reined in expansion in its core business, convinced that the U.S. market was saturated. Its chairman, Robert Dewar, created a special strategy group whose purpose was to study new growth avenues and, in the parlance of the time, far-out ideas. He also established a performance goal for the company: 25% of sales should come from new ventures by 1990.

What's most disturbing about Kmart's choices is not that management was tempted to diversify in search of growth—however misguided this appears in hindsight, given Wal-Mart's concurrent gathering of strength. Rather, it is that the executive team failed to monitor and match the distribution and inventory management capabilities that its rival was pioneering in Bentonville, Arkansas. In the early 1980s, while Wal-Mart was installing its first point-of-service system with a satellite link for automatic reorders, Kmart was acquiring Furr's Cafeterias of Texas, the Bishop's Buffet chain, and pizza-video parlors as outlets for its retained earnings. Throughout the next decade Wal-Mart continued to invest in its cross-docking distribution system, while Kmart pursued a range of disparate businesses, including PayLess Drug Stores, the Sports Authority, and Office-Max. By the end of the 1980s Kmart was at least 10 years behind Wal-Mart in its logistical capabilities, handing Wal-Mart a "gimme" advantage of more than 1% of sales in inbound logistics costs. As Kmart lagged ever further behind, its imagined need for outside-the-core growth platforms became real.

Of all the red flags signaling stall risk, one of the most obvious is management's use of the term "mature" to refer to any of its product lines, business units, or divisions. (The disinvestment in the core implied by the "cash cow" cell of the growth-share matrix does modern managers no favor.) Established businesses should be managed against significant revenue and earnings goals, and business leaders should actively explore the potential of new business models to rejuvenate even the most "mature" businesses.

When Talent Comes Up Short

Our fourth major category is talent bench shortfall: a lack of leaders and staff with the skills and capabilities required for strategy execution.

Talent bench shortfall merits careful definition, because it has become a fact of daily life in many industries and functions. Indeed, at this writing, shortages of critical talent are the primary concern of human resources departments globally, not just in high-growth markets but in a range of specialty skill categories, and they are expected to get worse. What stops growth dead in its tracks, however, is not merely a shortage of talent but the absence of required capabilities—such as solutions-selling skills or consumer-marketing expertise—in key areas of a company, most visibly at the executive level.

Internal skill gaps are often self-inflicted wounds, the unintended consequence of promote-from-within policies that have been too strictly applied. Such policies, often most fervent in organizations with strong cultures, can accelerate growth in the heady early days of executing a successful business model. But when the external environment presents novel challenges, or competition intensifies, these policies may be a severe drag on progress.

One important element in this category is a narrow experience base at the senior executive level that prevents a timely response to emerging strategic issues. The most common marker of this lack of experience is managers' tendency to follow a well-worn internal path from a dominant business, market, or function to the executive suite. Hitachi, which went into a growth stall in 1994, illustrates this problem. At the time, Hitachi accounted for 2% of Japan's GNP and 6% of its corporate R&D spending. The downward slide in the company's revenue was devastating. Executive management has consistently come up from the energy and industrial side of the company, but Hitachi's growth prospects lie elsewhere. This narrowness extends to functional pedigree: The firm has historically had an engineering culture, with none of its top executives holding an MBA or other business degree. As Hitachi looks toward its centennial in 2010, however, change may be in the offing: Kazuo Furukawa, who was named president and chief operating officer in 2006, came up through the telecom and information systems sectors. He is the company's first president with no exposure to its heavy electrical machinery business.

Few companies formally monitor the balance in the executive team between company lifers and newer hires who offer fresh perspectives and approaches. Furthermore, large companies have a fairly poor track record on incorporating new voices into senior management. Most studies agree that 35% to 40% of senior hires wash out within their first 18 months—a statistic that is improving glacially as we adopt new practices in talent management. And management development programs all too often focus on replicating the skill sets of the current leadership, rather than on developing the novel skills and perspectives that tomorrow's leaders will need to overcome evolving challenges.

We have identified a simple way to ensure balance in the senior executive ranks—what we call mix management. Our analysis of company growth rates and senior leaders' backgrounds suggests that the sweet spot for external talent is somewhere between 10% and 30% of senior management. That is a good target for the CEO and the board to use with the firm's executive committee and for human resources to use with the top 5% of the workforce.

When What You Know Is No Longer So

As noted, the four categories we have outlined account for nearly half of all the root causes we cataloged. A host of other, less common causes that came up in our analysis crossed a broad terrain, including failed acquisitions, key customer dependency, strategic diffusion, adjacency failures, and voluntary growth slowdowns. A powerful observation can be distilled from this array: One culprit in all our case studies was management's failure to bring the underlying assumptions that drive company strategy into line with changes in the external environment—whether because of a lack of awareness that the gap existed or was widening, or because of faulty prioritization.

The lack of awareness is particularly vexing, because it is so insidious. Strategic assumptions begin life as observations about customers, competitors, or technologies that arise from direct experience. They are then enshrined in the strategic plan and translated into

operational guidance. Eventually they harden into ortho-
doxy. This explains why, when we examine individual
case studies, we so often find that those assumptions the
team has held the longest or the most deeply are the like-
liest to be its undoing. Some beliefs have come to appear
so obvious that it is no longer politic to debate them.

Part of the reason that few top teams question
assumptions is that doing so goes against the nature of
the senior executive mandate: The CEO and his or her
executive team are paid to develop a vision and execute
it—with resolve. Another part is human nature: Intro-
spection and self-doubt don't often appear in the personality profiles of top executives at large enterprises. A
third part is process: CEOs have very few opportunities
to safely express their midnight anxieties. And the one
opportunity for stock taking that is built into the annual
calendar of most firms—the review of the strategic plan
for the coming year—all too often fails to stimulate deep,
searching conversation. Indeed, the "assumptions and
risks" section of virtually all strategic plan templates is
generally treated as a pro forma exercise rather than an
occasion to go deep.

Articulating and Testing Strategic Assumptions

To assist executives in spotting signs of vulnerability to
growth stalls in their own organizations, we offer two
kinds of tools. The first is a diagnostic self-test we developed at the conclusion of our research. Hoping to determine how companies might foresee a stall, our team
spent considerable time looking at various financial metrics, from margin erosion to patterns in R&D spending.
This effort was fruitless: Financial metrics—at least

those available to the public—are as likely to lag behind as lead an organization's change in strategic vitality.

What we did find helpful was asking, What could the company's senior managers have seen in their markets, in their competitors' behavior, in their own internal practices, that might have alerted them to an impending stall? We looked at our detailed case histories for warning signs before the stall point that perhaps hadn't received the scrutiny they deserved, and uncovered 50 red flags, all rooted in the real experience of the companies we studied. Our 20/20 hindsight may enable you to spot signs faster in your own organization. (See "Red Flags for Growth Stalls" at the end of this article.)

Also included in our tool kit are four practices drawn from those we've seen management teams use. The first two are effective in making strategic assumptions explicit, and the latter two are designed to test those assumptions for ongoing relevance and accuracy. A hallmark of these practices is that they are embedded in the work flow of the firm—the job of some individual or team—or otherwise built into core operating systems.

COMMISSION A CORE-BELIEF IDENTIFICATION SQUAD

This practice is simple to execute and involves calling on a diverse, cross-functional working group to go hunting for the firm's most deeply held assumptions about itself and the industry in which it operates. (Gary Hamel and his colleagues at Strategos have led the way on this practice.) The best-functioning squads include a significant share of younger, newer employees, who are less likely to be invested in current orthodoxies. Their efforts are most fruitful when the team is prepared to raise thorny issues and challenge entrenched beliefs, using methods ranging from reality checks—What industry are we in? Who are our customers?—to more provocative explorations: What 10 things would you never hear customers say about our business? Which firms have succeeded by breaking the established "rules" of the industry? What conventions did they overturn?

One leading consumer-goods company told us that it had used this practice to kick off an inquiry into long-term growth pathways and to challenge conventions that had taken hold through the years. We like the practice for two reasons. First, it seems to strike the right balance between traditional, closed-door strategy discussions and all-company "jams," which tend to lose credibility and edge in direct proportion to the number of participants involved. Second, it manages to simultaneously address areas of universal agreement and issues that are in play.

CONDUCT A PREMORTEM STRATEGIC ANALYSIS

Many leaders have found it useful to charge teams with developing competing visions of the future success—or failure—of the company as it would be reported in a business periodical five years hence. (See Gary Klein, "Performing a Project *Pre*mortem," Forethought, HBR September 2007.) The process typically takes place over one or two days at regularly scheduled offsite management gatherings, and teams senior executives with high-potential staffers from around the world. By seeing which issues the scenarios have in common, leadership teams can identify the subset of core beliefs that should be most closely examined and monitored.

APPOINT A SHADOW CABINET

Pioneered by a *Fortune* 250 manufacturing company, the shadow cabinet is a standing group of high-potential employees who tend to be in midcareer and are often in line for promotion to the director level. They usually meet the day before an executive committee meeting, and their agenda matches as closely as possible the agenda for the following day, with presenters delivering dry runs of their material to the group and then providing whatever follow-up is needed to support the group's deliberations and decision making. The members of the shadow cabinet are invited to executive committee meetings on a rotating basis.

The benefits of this practice are manifold. Because it provides such powerful seasoning for the employees who participate, it becomes a mainstay of the leadership development curriculum. And because senior executives are usually most attached to the assumptions underlying current strategy (it is *their* strategy, after all), they find the fresh perspectives offered by this creditable, well-informed constituency extremely valuable. That said, most executives to whom we've presented this idea respond that it would never work in their organizations. "The executive agenda is too confidential," they say, or "Our executive team is too impatient," or "It looks like too much work." We agree that this practice is not for everyone; in fact, we have visited boardrooms where speaking candidly about shortcomings in company strategy would be a truly career-limiting move. Organizations where this is the case should pass on the idea. Not only will it fail to achieve the desired effect but it may cause more harm than good to the morale of staff members involved in the initiative.

INVITE A VENTURE CAPITALIST TO YOUR STRATEGY REVIEW

An effective way to bring an external perspective to bear on strategy assumptions is to ask a qualified venture capitalist to sit in on business unit strategy and investment reviews and probe for potential weaknesses. The benefits for business unit managers come primarily from specific challenges but more generally from the practical, payback-focused lens that the VC brings to the review. What's more, the impact of the venture capitalist approach can live on well after the exercise. (Recording all the questions and methods the VC uses to gather information will preserve the essentials of the approach for later reuse.)

The obvious difficulty in implementing this practice is identifying an external party who is knowledgeable enough to add value to the conversation but "safe" enough to be allowed in the room. (In the current climate, representatives from the private equity community might easily meet the first requirement but miserably fail the second.) The organization that brought this idea to our attention was coventuring with a VC and so had begun to build some operating trust.

Unlike corporate investors, VCs are accustomed to serving on the boards of portfolio companies; acting in a similar capacity for a corporate partner isn't much of a stretch. For the corporate partner, however, the experience can be nothing short of eye-opening. The VC's perspective provides an in-the-moment test of assumptions about markets, customers, and competitors and brings an urgency to corporate processes that often feel routine. Deliberation around investment proposals takes on a very different tone. For a venture capitalist, each decision to fund is optional; the usual approach is to release

additional funding only when meaningful milestones
have been achieved. Freedom to operate for a quarter—
not a year—is the norm.

Renewing Competence in Strategy

The practices we recommend in this article compete for
space on an already overcrowded executive agenda.
What gives force to our advocacy is that growth stalls
can have dire consequences: They bring down even the
most admired companies; they exact a sizable financial
and human toll; and their impact may be permanent.
After a stall sets in, the odds against recovery rise dramatically with the passage of time. (See the exhibit "The
Long-Term Effects of Stalls.")

Compounding this urgency, all signs point to an
increasing risk of stalls in the near future. Of particular
concern today is the shrinking half-life of established
business models. The importance of spotting change
early enough to react in time is rising exponentially. The
practices we outline here create that early-warning capability. As critical, they make the strategy conversation
ongoing, rather than once a quarter or once a year, and
charge line managers at all levels of the firm with leading
that conversation. Clay Christensen argued in these
pages a decade ago that competent strategic thinking
was atrophying in the executive suite because it occurred
so infrequently relative to other regular activities. (See
"Making Strategy: Learning by Doing," HBR November–
December 1997.) As students of strategy-making in large
corporations since then, we have found that the problem
has only worsened.

Whatever other concerns are on the strategy agenda,
guarding against growth stalls should be at the top.
The tools we offer will enable the executive team to

continually test the accuracy of its worldview and to flag any flawed assumptions that might trigger a stall if they go uncorrected. We know of no more powerful investment for managing controllable risk.

The Long-Term Effects of Stalls

Fortune 100 and Global 100 Companies, 1955–2006

The overwhelming majority (87%) of companies in our study had experienced a stall. Fewer than half of those (4.6%) were able to return to moderate or high growth within the decade. When slow growth was allowed to persist for more than 10 years, the delay was most often fatal: Only 7% of the companies in that category ever returned to moderate or high growth.

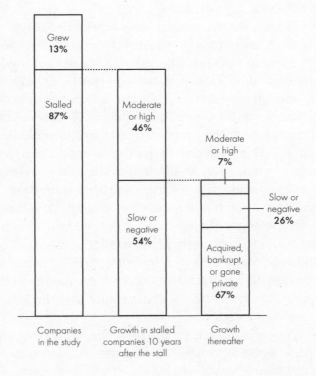

The Search for Stall Points

TO UNDERSTAND THE PREVALENCE of serious growth crises in large companies, as well as their costs and causes, we analyzed the experiences of more than 400 companies that have been listed on the *Fortune* 100 since its inception, in 1955, and of about 90 comparable non-U.S. companies. Some 500 companies over 50 years gave us 25,000 years' worth of historical data and information to mine for insights. A pattern that emerged from these histories yielded the useful construct of the stall point—that moment when a company's growth rate slips into what proves to be a prolonged decline.

We began by analyzing the revenue growth records of every company in our study to identify which companies had experienced stall points and when. Specifically, we calculated the compound annual growth rate (CAGR) of each company's revenue for 10 years before and 10 years after every year in the past half-century for which data were available. To qualify as having stalled in a given year, a company must have enjoyed compound annual growth of at least 2% in real dollars for the 10-year period prior to the potential stall point; the difference in CAGR for the 10 years preceding and the 10 years following must have been at least four percentage points; and the CAGR of the subsequent 10 years must have fallen below 6% in real dollars. One stall point identified in this manner is shown in the chart.

We then turned our attention to *why* companies stall. Out of the 500 companies, we selected for in-depth case research 50 that were representative of the whole in terms of industry mix and age. We assembled comprehensive dossiers on all of them, drawing on the public record of financial reports and published materials, on case studies, and on personal interviews. This enabled us to identify the top three factors contributing to each company's growth stall. After all these analyses we were able to identify the root causes of stalls and the major categories they fell into. We arrived at our framework purely inductively, from the bottom up. (See "The Root Causes of Revenue Stalls" earlier in this article.)

Readers may be wondering why we chose revenue rather than profit, value, or some other measure on which to focus our analysis. That is a fair question, and we considered our choice at length. It rests on two premises. The first is that revenue growth, more than any other metric, is the primary driver of long-term company performance. This is not to say that revenue growth without profits is desirable, but high growth through margin management alone is unsustainable. The second premise is more mundane: It's hard to manipulate the top line over time, and market value and profit measures are much more variable. Revenue growth guided us to the most meaningful turning points in corporate growth history.

We would be pleased to discuss any aspect of this methodology or detail of our findings with analysts wishing to learn more or to replicate our approach. We maintain an updated list of FAQs about this initiative on our website, at www.stallpoints.executiveboard.com.

One Company's Stall Point

TRACKING THE GROWTH OF the BF Goodrich Corporation over a 20-year period, we can clearly see its stall point. Annual growth rates are shown for a decade before and a decade after what proved to be the stall year. The turning point in Goodrich's fortunes came in 1979, after which the company's growth fell into secular decline.

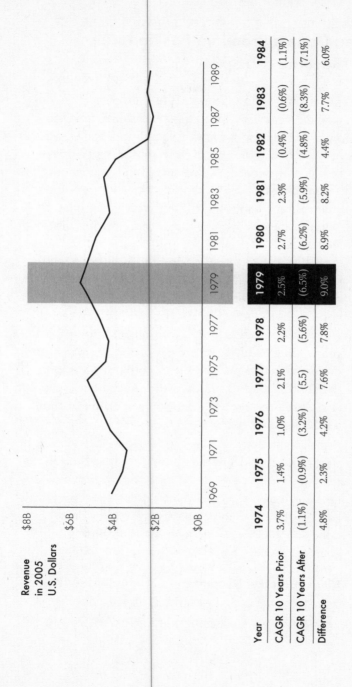

Year	1974	1975	1976	1977	1978	1979	1980	1981	1982	1983	1984
CAGR 10 Years Prior	3.7%	1.4%	1.0%	2.1%	2.2%	2.5%	2.7%	2.3%	(0.4%)	(0.6%)	(1.1%)
CAGR 10 Years After	(1.1%)	(0.9%)	(3.2%)	(5.5)	(5.6%)	(6.5%)	(6.2%)	(5.9%)	(4.8%)	(8.3%)	(7.1%)
Difference	4.8%	2.3%	4.2%	7.6%	7.8%	9.0%	8.9%	8.2%	4.4%	7.7%	6.0%

When Does a Premium Position Become a Trap?

AT THE TOP OF EVERY INDUSTRY are companies that have built premium positions for themselves, dominating the market among the most demanding customer segments and providing products or services that lead the field in performance, thus commanding higher prices. The organizational strengths in product development, brand management, and marketing that created these top positions are sources of great pride to the firms that cultivated them.

But attack from new competitors with significantly lower cost structures, or changes in customer preferences that start slowly and then reach tipping points, can actually transform these dependable sources of competitive advantage into weaknesses. Product innovation loses its ability to protect pricing premiums, and presumed brand and marketing strengths no longer dependably protect market share. All the firm's business processes and activities, developed and honed for the top end of the market, become impediments to refreshing strategy.

It is possible to spot the onset of premium-position captivity. The six yes-or-no questions below probe awareness of threatening market dynamics, an executive team's blind spots regarding competitive threats, and intelligence capabilities for recognizing an impending encroachment on premium turf.

Clues in Market Dynamics

- Are we losing market share to nonpremium rivals in subsegments of our markets?

- Are key customers increasingly resistant to paying price premiums for product enhancements?

Clues in Executive Team Attitudes

- Does the senior executive team resist the proposition that nonpremium players operate in the same business or product category that we do?
- Do we commonly dismiss the possibility that nonpremium rivals and low-end entrants will penetrate the upper ends of our markets?

Clues in Market and Competitor Research

- Do we fail to track shifts in secondary and tertiary customer-group behavior with the same rigor we use for our higher-end segments?
- Do we exclude nonpremium players and low-end entrants from our tracking of competitive threats?

A "yes" to two or more of these questions suggests the need to refocus research into markets and competitors. The goal should be to map premium features and low-end competitor performance. A "yes" to four or more suggests an immediate need for contingency planning: How might the firm modify its current business model (including its margin requirements and cost basis) to respond to a low-cost entrant within 18 months?

Red Flags for Growth Stalls

ARE YOU ABOUT TO HIT a stall point? A diagnostic survey of 50 red flags can help signal the danger in time. Below is a sampling of red flags relating to premium-position captivity; other parts of the survey highlight other hazards. To the extent that your senior team and high-potential managers see these as areas for concern, you may be headed for a free fall.

- Our core assumptions about the marketplace and about the capabilities that are critical to support our strategy are not written down.

- We haven't revisited our market definition boundaries, and therefore our list of current and emerging competitors, in several years.

- We haven't refreshed our working definition of our core market, and therefore our understanding of our market share, in several years.

- We test only infrequently for shifts in key customer groups' valuation of our product/service attributes.

- We are less effective than our competitors at translating customer insights into new product and service categories.

- Core customers are increasingly unwilling to pay a premium for our brand reputation or superior performance.

  To watch the authors discuss their complete list of red flags and how to use them to diagnose impending growth stalls, go to stallpoints.multimedia.hbr.org. There you can link to the full diagnostic survey, at www.stallpoints.executiveboard.com.

Originally published in March 2008
Reprint R0803C

Leadership and the Psychology of Turnarounds

ROSABETH MOSS KANTER

Executive Summary

TURNAROUND CHAMPIONS—those leaders who manage to bring distressed organizations back from the brink of failure—are often acclaimed for their canny financial and strategic decision making. But having studied their work closely, Harvard Business School's Rosabeth Moss Kanter emphasizes another aspect of their achievement. These leaders reverse the cycle of corporate decline through deliberate interventions that increase the level of communication, collaboration, and respect among their managers.

Ailing companies descend into what Kanter calls a "death spiral," which typically works this way: After an initial blow to the company's fortunes, people begin pointing fingers and deriding colleagues in other parts of the business. Tensions rise and collaboration declines. Once they are no longer acting in concert, people find themselves less able to effect change. Eventually, many come to believe they are helpless. Passivity sets in. Finally, the ultimate pathology of troubled companies takes hold: denial. Rather than volunteer an opinion that no one else seems to share, people engage in collective pretense to ignore what they individually know.

To counter these dynamics, Kanter says, and reverse the company's slide, the CEO needs to apply certain psychological interventions—specifically, replacing secrecy and denial with dialogue, blame and scorn with respect, avoidance and turf protection with collaboration, and passivity and helplessness with initiative. The author offers in-depth accounts of how the CEOs at Gillette, Invensys, and the BBC used these interventions to guide their employees out of corporate free fall and onto a more productive path.

IN RECENT YEARS, I have been inside nearly two dozen turnaround situations, in various stages of progress, in which new leaders were bringing distressed organizations back from the brink of failure and setting them on a healthier course. In every case, I saw—and agreed with—the need for smart financial and strategic decision making. But along the way, I also noted another important aspect of this leadership task, a related line of effort that seemed to go largely unnoticed and unstudied by observers but that was just as vital to improving the company's fortunes and just as hard to do well. Each of these executives restored their people's confidence in themselves and in one another—a necessary antecedent to restoring investor or public confidence. They inspired and empowered their organizations to take new actions that could renew profitability. In short, each had to lead a psychological turnaround.

Consider the situations that confronted new CEOs in three companies:

Gillette: Its performance was strong through the mid-1990s, but by the beginning of 2001, this global consumer-products company had experienced several years of flat sales, declining operating margins, and loss of market share. Its Mach3 shaving system was a block-buster product, but the company was suffering the effects of its own reliance on trade loading—the practice of offering discounts to retail customers at the end of a quarter in order to move products and achieve sales targets, thus sacrificing margins and jeopardizing the next quarter's sales. Meanwhile, because the executives in different product groups and locations rarely sat in the same meetings, initiatives in their various areas were not coordinated. SKUs (stockkeeping units, or product variations) proliferated as groups made decisions without informing other departments, leading to waste and duplication. Respect among peers declined.

BBC: In 1999, the British Broadcasting Corporation was a seriously demoralized organization. Its funding was secure through 2006 because of a government-collected licensing fee, but it had lost audience share, experienced declining ratings, and was being outpaced by commercial competitors. Skepticism and cynicism reigned in the company. Many people felt under attack, externally and internally. Program developers felt they were at the mercy of broadcast commissioners and that they were being treated unfairly, having to endure a long bureaucratic process that ended in their show proposals being rejected more than half the time. The radio division felt it didn't get the same respect as the TV unit. The sports division had to fight for airtime. Employees regularly went to the press to air grievances, reinforcing the BBC's culture of blame.

Invensys: A global conglomerate that was created largely through acquisitions, Invensys in 2001 had more than 50,000 people working in industrial and energy services—and was close to defaulting on its financial obligations. Some managers felt the company was also bankrupt in terms of ideas. There was insufficient communication across the company, including few common meetings of the top group, competition among divisions that were largely isolated from one another, and an inward focus among managers. Perpetual restructuring had created a culture of fear and had reduced employee initiative. When the new CEO asked executives individually to name the three people in the company for whom they had the greatest respect, most could barely name one.

It may be true, to paraphrase Tolstoy, that every unhappy organization is unhappy in its own way, but once we set aside the details, the fundamental dynamics of decline—and recovery from it—in these three companies turn out to be remarkably similar. Indeed, across a wide variety of situations, in banking, consumer products, retail, industrial products, software, education, and media in North America and Europe, I've found the same pattern. Organizational pathologies—secrecy, blame, isolation, avoidance, passivity, and feelings of helplessness—arise during a difficult time for the company and reinforce one another in such a way that the company enters a kind of death spiral. Reversing that downward trend requires deliberate efforts by the CEO to address each of the pathologies.

Here's how this spiraling effect worked at a company I'll call Industrial Era Corporation, or IEC.

The Dynamics of Decline:
A View from Inside

IEC was once a rapidly growing industry darling. But a series of lackluster products and expenses too high for a shrinking post-tech-crash market had set it on a downward path. Meanwhile, its largest rival went from strength to strength in the same unforgiving market. It was almost as if they were now two different species. The rival could do no wrong; IEC could do no right. One analyst declared that IEC was worth more dead than alive. Institutional customers called to ask whether the company would be able to meet service commitments to its products. Each group that questioned IEC's viability caused other groups to lose confidence.

IEC tried to bounce back by launching two innovative products. But neither moved the company off the death watch, because everything IEC did was now viewed as evidence of weakness. The organization was under a negative halo. Psychologists define the halo effect as the aura that surrounds a successful person or organization. Indeed, when IEC was on the rise, its founders were lionized as brilliant strategists, and the praise heaped on IEC made its products more desirable and reinforced a growth spiral. The halo effect had hidden any weaknesses back then. Now it was hiding IEC's strengths.

When IEC posted a string of consecutive quarters of decline, the company's leaders thought they could push their way back into the black by exhorting people to reduce their expenses further and launch new products faster. Commands started flowing from the top. But the tighter controls were greeted with cynicism. Some people began to do the minimum, showing up at work just long enough to earn their end-of-year bonus. Managers distanced themselves from company decisions. They would tell outside consultants that they weren't involved, that they disagreed with the decisions, or that someone else in another division or department was responsible.

As problems mounted, so did the likelihood of secrecy and isolation among managers. People tended to either blame or avoid one another. Since bad news is never as welcome as good news, and there was more bad news than good, IEC managers kept communications with the staff and one another to the bare minimum. It wasn't that they were consciously hiding problems; they simply found reasons to cancel or postpone meetings, often citing increased work pressures.

The CEO told managers to focus on improving their own performance, and he put their bonuses at risk. As group heads emphasized meeting current targets, the company virtually eliminated cross-functional or cross-division projects. Groups knew less about what was going on in other parts of the organization and stopped caring—or cared too much, imagining how others might be plotting to cut them out of their share of a shrinking budget. Various business efforts were duplicated; each group felt it was easier to perform tasks itself rather than coordinate its actions with others.

Increasingly, people's time and energy were spent on self-protection instead of joint problem solving. The invisible walls between territories grew. Most senior executives at IEC sat within a few feet of one another in offices with glass walls, yet many professed ignorance of the other units' plans to solve IEC's problems. The CEO and CFO tended to control the information that circulated. Though reporting requirements increased during IEC's troubled period, communication outside of formal meetings decreased.

It became rare for all the senior executives to sit down in one room together. Executives found reasons not to attend meetings because those few meetings that remained had degenerated into diatribes by the CEO, followed by uninformative reports. No one wanted to raise questions because that tended to produce angry exchanges, as department heads accused other department heads of putting obstacles in their paths. The game became one of blaming others before they could blame you. For example, the head of IEC's customer service group wrote memos outlining the problems other divisions were causing that his department had to fix. Since the good performers in the organization did not want to be tainted by the failure of the poor performers, those in units with strong sales became openly scornful of their peers in other units.

Managers with opportunities were leaving. Not all the departures were mourned; some senior managers had not met expectations. But now IEC was constantly recruiting to fill holes at the top, and critical tasks were left undone because executives were on double duty—for example, the CIO was now supervising the operations group. All of this reinforced the dynamics of IEC's decline. Employees had so little interest in socializing with one another outside of work that the CEO had to order his direct reports to show up at a company social event.

To cope with the decline, IEC got caught in the trade-loading trap, common in troubled companies. Toward the end of each quarter, IEC offered promotional deals to its distributors to move inventory. This was a tantalizingly simple short-run solution to declining sales but tended to make the situation worse. The price cuts reduced the funds available for marketing, which increased IEC's reliance on the promotional deals. And customers knew they could wait until quarter's end to get even better deals. IEC's managers felt they had no

choice but to continue to discount. Acting from a weak
bargaining position reinforced IEC's ever-weakening
position.

That assumption of weakness reflects a phenomenon
psychologists call learned helplessness, a term coined by
the University of Pennsylvania's Martin Seligman. Many
people at IEC began to feel there was little they could do
to make a difference in the company's fortunes. They
became passive. The CEO complained that he had to
come up with all the good ideas; the more he complained, the worse people felt about their own ideas,
since presumably theirs weren't the good ones. Managers
set low goals to guarantee they would achieve them. One
group at IEC tested a new method for selling products
that had doubled sales, but other managers wrote much
lower numbers into their plans in case the new method
wouldn't work for them. Think of this as the opposite of
the arrogance of success—it's the timidity of mediocrity.
Individual choices, each logical to the person making it,
added up to a system that caused people to feel power-
less. And the downward cycle continued.

Reversing the Cycle

IEC's story demonstrates how problem fuels problem in
an ailing organization's culture. (See the exhibit "The
Troubled Company's Cycle of Decline.") The dynamic
boils down to this: After an initial blow to the company's
fortunes, people begin pointing fingers and deriding colleagues in other parts of the business. The resulting tensions curtail collaboration and degenerate quickly into
turf protection. Increasing levels of isolation throughout
the company then engender secrecy. Once they are no
longer acting in concert, people find themselves less able

The Troubled Company's Cycle of Decline

Corporate decline generally does not stem from a single factor; it results from an accumulation of decisions, actions, and commitments that become entangled in self-perpetuating workplace dynamics. Secrecy, blame, isolation, avoidance, lack of respect, and feelings of helplessness create a culture that makes an already bad situation worse. Once a company is caught in this spiral, it is hard to simply stop and reverse direction. The system has momentum, and change seems impossible. But there are interventions managers can use to shift the momentum in the company's favor.

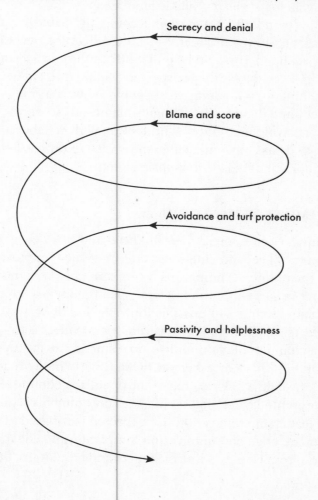

Secrecy and denial

Blame and score

Avoidance and turf protection

Passivity and helplessness

to effect change, and eventually many come to believe they are helpless. Passivity sets in. Finally, the ultimate pathology of troubled companies takes hold: collective denial. As in the fabled village where the emperor showed off his new clothes, people unwittingly collude. Rather than volunteer an opinion that no one else seems to share, people engage in collective pretense to ignore what they individually know. It's a phenomenon known to psychologists as pluralistic ignorance.

How wonderful, then, when a company is able to pull out of that downward spiral—as IEC did after a new CEO took the helm. How did he pull it off? In the end, the only way a CEO can reverse a corporate decline is to change the momentum and empower people anew, replacing secrecy and denial with dialogue, blame and scorn with respect, avoidance and turf protection with collaboration, and passivity and helplessness with initiative. Let's look at each of these interventions in turn.

PROMOTING DIALOGUE

Companies compound their financial and strategic woes when they keep information secret from their employees and the public. As numerous recent scandals have made clear, the cover-up is often worse than the mistake. And problem solving is impossible if people do not have all the facts. So the first task of turnaround leaders is to open channels of communication—starting at the top.

On Jim Kilts's first day as CEO of Gillette in February 2001, he held a full meeting of the operating committee. He presented a detailed set of slides outlining his style and leadership philosophy. He expected fact-based management, open communication, simplicity, and collaboration from Gillette's line managers and employees. Featured prominently on the list titled "My Style" was the statement, "If something bothers you, I want open dialogue." Kilts then outlined the results of his month-long external review of the company prior to joining, a detailed analysis of Gillette's strengths and weaknesses. He was also planning to present this information to the board several days later. Kilts immediately established multiple communication channels—weekly staff meetings, weekly business overviews from all executives worldwide, quarterly two-day off-site meetings for senior executives, a chairman's page on Gillette's intranet where anyone in the company could post questions and receive answers from Kilts himself, the distribution of videotaped dialogues with Kilts for managers in the international locations he couldn't visit personally, and employee roundtables.

One of Kilts's more controversial moves, but one that increased disclosure among colleagues at Gillette and pushed communications forward, was to expose the performance data regarding his top team. The CEO introduced quarterly report cards for his senior managers, and after the first ones were completed, he posted the results for the whole top team to see (anonymously at first) so that everyone knew where they stood in relation to their peers. Those scorecards were followed by senior managers' open presentations of their priorities for the next quarter. Secrecy and denial were relegated to the trash bin; there was no way to hide information.

The nature of conversations at Gillette shifted from individual reports to group dialogue. Previously, managers told me, they would go to meetings, say their piece, and go away. With Kilts at the helm, managers said their piece—and stayed to answer questions. "He does not attempt to wrap himself or the company in any sort of mystical qualities," an executive observed. Anything was open for questioning.

Almost identical shifts in quantity and quality of communication occurred in the other companies I observed. At the BBC, new CEO Greg Dyke restructured to remove a layer of the organization that had stood between top management and those responsible for audiences and products (the broadcasters and show producers). He put program people on the executive committee and gave them a voice in decisions. Meetings became more frequent and much more informal. Dyke favored open and direct communication through personal e-mails to individual employees as well as broadcasts to the whole of the BBC. The BBC's finance director noted, "He writes the messages himself, to everyone, from the heart, telling the truth, telling people what he wants them to do, and communicating instantaneously." Dyke also sought less formality among senior managers so they could spend more time talking about strategic issues. Dyke reduced the divisions' formal reporting requirements to the executive committee. BBC News had previously submitted status updates in six three-inch binders; Dyke condensed the requirements so that the reports fit on ten pages. Staffers often remarked about the CEO's personal warmth. An executive said, "Greg cares about people— he touches them on the shoulder and arm—a sharp contrast from the behavior of most standoffish Brits. He establishes a connection and makes time for as many people as possible."

CEO Rick Haythornthwaite and his team made dialogue a hallmark of the new Invensys. Town-hall–type meetings were convened in the largest of the company's 400 sites worldwide. Haythornthwaite picked up the phone to call people who raised an interesting point or a

note of dissent on the company's "Ask Rick" help line.
And he still continues to be personally involved in the
drafting of responses to employee questions. Dialogue
means that everyone deserves a response. "If you do drop
the ball, people know about it very quickly," Haythornthwaite said. "And even though it creates an incredible
amount of pressure, you've got to be thinking every day,
Is there someone I cut short? Is there something that
someone said in a meeting that I haven't followed up?
Those things just undermine the effort."

In a company where there was a perceived distance
between the leadership and the workforce, Haythornthwaite made a point of standing before his employees
with no podium between him and them. At one town
hall meeting, he spoke about company issues in front of
what felt like a factory floor of humanity. When it was
time for questions, the first person asked him why the
company had trimmed the health plan. "It was one of
those moments where you could see everything was
hanging on my answer," Haythornthwaite recalled. "I
hadn't even been responsible for the decision, so I could
have said that it wasn't me, that it was the previous
guys." Instead, Haythornthwaite acknowledged that the
decision wasn't his—but that he was accountable for the
fallout. He presented the facts about the costs of the
health plan. Given those facts, the crowd could see that
cutting from the health plan was the only sensible course
of action. "The only way I could give you a different
answer is by fundamentally shifting the U.S. health care
system," he told the group, and at that point the audience was back on his side. "People just hadn't been
treated to the facts in the past. That's just so consciously
condescending. If you're all in the same game, then you
share those facts."

ENGENDERING RESPECT

Open dialogue exposes facts and tells the truth, but a successful corporate turnaround depends on relationships as well as information. It is very tempting for a new regime to exact revenge and punish those responsible for past mistakes. But that would only guarantee that organizational pathologies—the company's blame culture—would continue. Turnaround leaders must move people toward respect; when colleagues respect one another's abilities, they are more likely to collaborate in shaping a better future. There is a parallel in the work of a great world leader. To turn around his country, Nelson Mandela, the first democratically elected president of South Africa, established a Truth and Reconciliation Commission. Reconciliation helps people move beyond assigning blame for problems; it helps them regain respect for one another while becoming more personally accountable.

Haythornthwaite was conscious of walking a fine line between truth and reconciliation. He observed, "You've got to speak to where the organization stands. And you've got to do it in a way that doesn't make people wrong but, at the same time, doesn't leave them in denial." He wanted to avoid punishing anyone for past mistakes, and he wanted to build mutual respect among colleagues. "You've got to create some space to make a mistake or two," he said. "We are but a collection of human beings." By making no changes in the senior-management ranks in his first months, except for one division head, Haythornthwaite signaled that there was quality to be found in the people already in the company. By involving about 100 people in strategy-formulation teams, he provided opportunities for them to demonstrate their talent. Haythornthwaite told them explicitly that he trusted them, that he believed there was talent in the company. At a three-day reporting session after their 45-day intensive effort to plot a new direction for Invensys, he said, "the mood was extraordinary. People we didn't know existed were offering high-quality presentations of strategic thinking. The overall level of respect for one another in the room rose." To set standards for a variety of processes, Invensys's new leaders looked inside the organization for best-in-class practices—among 53,000 people there were surely examples of best practice—as another way to raise organizational esteem and confidence.

Similarly, Jim Kilts's initial actions at Gillette helped people look at the facts without becoming defensive about them. Kilts's message from day one was that he had no preconceived notions about people and no plans to make sweeping changes in the management ranks. "We have a very good cadre of people who want to do the right thing," he said. One of his priorities was to eliminate the finger-pointing that had gone on in the past. Frequent meetings among managers who never had much of an opportunity to sit together before made this possible. If an executive said he did not reach a certain target because someone else didn't do his part, Kilts would turn to that person to ask what happened and to remind everyone of the overarching objectives and priorities linking the areas. A participant recalled that the first quarterly off-site under Kilts was tension ridden, with outbursts of anger as people played out the blame culture of the past. But over time, the meetings became more effective and team oriented. "I don't want competition among functions or the senior staff. Anything that even hints at it is counterproductive. I hate anyone saying 'Jim said' or 'Jim wants' or 'the board said' or 'the board wants' as the reason for doing or not doing something. Things are done, or not, based on rigorous assessments and considered deliberations," Kilts said. That also meant that people could start relying on each other to be accountable.

It is hard to play politics if everything is discussed openly. The BBC's Greg Dyke changed the tone and style of the executive committee meetings dramatically. An executive explained, "In the past, managers would lobby the director general privately, so you would go into a meeting and not know where you stood. With Greg, if you have any issue, it needs to be put on the table. Meetings are more chatty, less formal, more sociable. We have away days. We do fun team-building events. We see each other socially." Dyke also expected managers to respect one another's ideas. To drive this home, he created yellow cards, resembling those used by referees to signal a penalty in soccer matches, labeled "Cut the Crap: Make It Happen." He used the cards himself, holding them up when he heard ideas getting trampled. BBC leaders started learning not to second-guess people but rather to extend trust.

At a leadership conference of several hundred people, a junior manager confessed in her small discussion group that she was out of pocket a few thousand pounds for a project because of BBC rules concerning qualified vendors and the timing of reimbursements. She was encouraged to speak up in the large group. After she described her situation, her boss offered to write her a check for the sum she awaited. But he was superseded by the BBC's finance director, who not only wrote the check but changed the rule on the spot.

SPARKING COLLABORATION

Turnaround leaders know that problem solving requires
collaboration across departments and divisions—and
not just because innovations often come from these joint
projects. Changing the company's dynamics requires collective commitments to new courses of action lest local
decisions, taken in isolation, undermine that change.
New strategies are possible when new kinds of conversations are held about combining organizational assets in
new ways. Thus, Greg Dyke's first major initiative,
announced within two months of his arrival, was called
"One BBC: Making It Happen," to highlight that he was
seeking more collaboration throughout the organization.
Executive committee meetings were increasingly
devoted to themes that cut across divisions, and members discovered areas in which they could combine
forces to tackle new business opportunities.

Gillette's complex organizational matrix meant that
many operations issues arose at the intersection of
groups—for instance, product managers required
resources and support from the IT department or needed
to coordinate their launches with help from sales representatives in the field. Jim Kilts encouraged the formation of operating committees in each business unit or
regional group, and then further encouraged the creation
of cross-matrix operating committees that included
representatives from all the functions and areas on
which the business unit depended. The view across the
organization revealed business opportunities that would
have been hard for any one unit to see by itself. For
example, Gillette's Oral-B business unit, centered in the
United States, produced a quality line of toothbrushes,
and its Braun division, headquartered in Germany, had

developed world-class portable-appliance technologies. But, unlike its competitors, Gillette did not make a battery-powered toothbrush—until new relationships were formed across the ocean.

Rather than continually reorganize, which is highly disruptive, especially for a troubled company, turn-around leaders simply augment the organization chart with flexible, often temporary, groups that open relation-ships in multiple directions. Invensys's Rick Haythorn-thwaite refers to this as structuring the organization to get the right discussions. "The only thing I really do is lead conversations," he says. "Any group is a network of conversations. I continuously thrust people into situa-tions that force them to challenge the current conversa-tion they're holding, to get beyond that discussion to one that's more productive."

Invensys's leadership team acted on this theory by adding new groups and roles, slicing through the organi-zation chart vertically, diagonally, and horizontally. In his first months at the company, Haythornthwaite formed nine strategy teams comprising people from across the divisions, with each team focused on one of nine customer segments. When the company launched this initiative, it involved the top 300 people in rank at the organization and 100 additional participants called "ambassadors for change," ensuring that people below the managerial ranks would be part of the strategy con-versation. Haythornthwaite also recruited experts to lead in four areas cutting across the business—supply chain (procurement), customer development, service delivery, and project management. They had only small teams and no P&L responsibility. Their charter was to set standards within their areas and to work with others to bring about necessary improvements.

INSPIRING INITIATIVE

Once turnaround CEOs establish the structures that allow people to collaborate, they need to empower their employees to initiate the actions that will improve the company's financial or strategic position. One incident at the BBC revealed that learned helplessness is a disease that even top executives can suffer and that initiative is not automatic even in those assumed to have power. Jane Root, controller of BBC2, remembered a pivotal executive committee meeting about a seemingly trivial matter: "Greg wanted to put up some posters on the wall and was told by someone on the executive committee that 'They won't allow that.' Greg said, 'Wait a moment—who won't allow it? We are them.' We had to break out of this infantilizing past. It took Greg to show us that we were in charge, that we could change things if we liked."

The push on the part of the executive committee to support new ideas and to collaborate on cross-division projects created some striking innovations at the BBC: a new time slot for the nightly TV news that boosted viewership; a successful Scottish soap opera produced locally rather than in London (the source of most programs in the past); and interactive features on the BBC Web site through the combined efforts of the news, sports, drama, and children's programming divisions. In another early win, a new trainee using funds intended for a training video created a ten-minute pilot for what became *The Office*, a hit comedy series about life in a dead-end, white-collar job.

The next step was to move idea generation from the BBC's executive committee and senior leaders to everyone in the company, ensuring a flow of ideas from the

bottom up as well as from the top down. At his annual
state-of-the-organization broadcast to the whole BBC in
February 2002, Greg Dyke announced the then-still-
unformed "One BBC" effort—but by now, the executive
committee was sufficiently confident that it could
announce a major initiative even if the details hadn't
been worked out. That was a major departure from the
committee's passive bureaucratic past. By July 2002,
5,000 people were involved in "One BBC: Making It Happen" brainstorming sessions; by November, 10,000 of the
BBC's 24,000 employees had participated. More than
2,000 ideas were submitted through the initiative's Web
site, and 700 had been implemented, including a BBC-
wide discount on digital set-top boxes and an important
new employee orientation program. Dyke personally
reviewed many of the proposals, and division managers
added their own support for grassroots innovations. BBC
Wales created a fund of £100,000 to pay for projects suggested by the staff, who then voted for the top seven
ideas; more than 900 people, 70% of the division, voted.

At Invensys, the leadership team conveyed the message that employees were now *expected* to show initiative. "The days of autocracy are over. You have to do it
yourself," Haythornthwaite told his people. The nine
strategy teams were a first step. Arming them with customer information, a framework, expert resources, dead-
line pressure (45 days), and a process, he left them to
develop the ideas themselves. A strategy rollout conference with the top 70 executives reflected their increasing
confidence and initiative. At one point, the Industrial
Components & Systems group walked out of the meeting, booked its own conference room, wrote a script for
divestitures, and returned with a sense of pride because
it had taken control.

Then Invensys started the long process of opening up the idea floodgates. The company created INVEST (identify, nominate, validate, evaluate, start, track), a program to find improvement projects already under way in the organization, as well as new ones, and give them a disciplined project-management process to make success more likely. "I want our 53,000 people to be able to come up with ideas that we'll be able to transform into results," Haythornthwaite said. A thousand INVEST team leaders were trained over six months by 33 master facilitators, and a Web-based system was developed to track the status of all the change programs. Haythornthwaite had to repeat the message several times for people to get on board, but then new opportunities popped up and old ones kept resurfacing—a virtual logjam of interconnected issues, from transfer pricing to incentive schemes. A new team was established to take action and to continue the process of empowerment.

The Energy for Change

Despite the common psychological dynamics at work in all the turnaround situations I've witnessed, we should remember that leading a corporate turnaround isn't a one-size-fits-all process. It requires that CEOs pay attention to the specifics of a company's problems and that the leaders bring their own preferred approaches to the task. Rick Haythornthwaite engaged large teams to work on a new strategy for Invensys, while Jim Kilts devised Gillette's strategy for each line of business by himself, working with a small group of trusted executives. Greg Dyke virtually eliminated consultants at the BBC to force managers to think for themselves, while Kilts retained many consultants to bring an external perspective to a company that had become too insular.

Yet, despite differences in strategies and tactics, all turnaround leaders share the overarching task of restoring confidence through empowerment—replacing denial with dialogue, blame with respect, isolation with collaboration, and helplessness with opportunities for initiative. Each leader must manage the tricky task of creating a winner's attitude in people, even before the victories.

And that means performing a series of balancing acts. Troubled organizations are generally in financial distress, and cutting expenses is a characteristic turnaround move. But how this is done has a big impact on whether the turnaround is a temporary fix or a path to sustainability. To pull a company out of a death spiral, the CEO needs to encourage people to take initiative and feel that they can make a difference—which is hard to achieve when an organization is in slash-and-burn mode. Effective turnaround leaders consider the kinds of cuts they're making as well as the number, emphasizing reductions in bureaucracy that stifles initiative, thus creating conditions for change. The BBC's Greg Dyke embarked on a campaign to reduce overhead over a five-year period, from 24% to 15% of revenues, by removing a level of management; cutting spending on consultants from £20 million a year to about £500,000 a year; and consolidating support functions and making it clear that such functions served the business units, not the other way around. The goal was not just a more efficient organization but one that invested in its products—broadcast channels and programs. Unlike previous rounds of cost cutting, this approach was not demoralizing; people at the BBC generally considered it empowering.

Invensys's Rick Haythornthwaite noted the enthusiasm with which people raised their aspirations and their performance. He said he was pleasantly surprised by "the quality of people that want to join. The people who don't think you're going to make it suddenly burst with enthusiasm, and then you've connected to something in their soul. It's a wonderful moment when you start having uplifting conversations. It's a pleasant surprise, the extent to which people are self-motivated." Restoring confidence raises aspirations, he told me. "And the gap between aspiration and business-as-usual is the source of energy for change."

One conclusion is unmistakable: Turnarounds are when leadership matters most. Managers can stem losses with a few bold strokes, such as slashing budgets or selling off assets. But putting an organization on a positive path toward future success also requires that leaders energize their workforce, throughout the ranks. The small wins that newly empowered people create are the first signs that a turnaround is on track. And this is the true test of leadership—whether those being led out of the defeatism of decline gain the confidence that produces victories.

A New Broom?

MOST OF THE EXEMPLARY turnaround leaders I've seen—including the CEOs of Gillette, the BBC, and Invensys—were new to their organizations as well as to their jobs. Does this mean that only a new broom can sweep clean?

Perhaps so. After all, if the old CEO had wrong ideas in the past, why should people believe he or she has the right idea now? Even when an executive who presided over a period of decline admits mistakes and embraces new ways, it's nearly impossible for that person to stir up the organizational energy needed for a turnaround. As former U.S. vice president Al Gore observed when he decided not to run for president in 2004, his candidacy undoubtedly would have been dogged by debate over why he lost the race in 2000, at a time when his party needed to focus relentlessly on moving forward.

But new CEOs have the edge in more positive ways, as well. They are better able to disentangle system dynamics because they were not caught up in them. For example, one of the most important steps of a psychological turnaround is putting a name to problems that have long gone unexpressed. At Gillette, for example, senior executives claimed to a person that they had known for years what the problems were: trade loading; long gaps between new product releases and a proliferation of minor upgrades on existing products; and the inappropriate application of the company's strategy for blades and razors to other categories, especially the Duracell battery business. As a Gillette group director for Europe proclaimed, "I'm absolutely certain there's not one person in the whole company who for one moment thought that we should do anything other than get out of trade loading." Yet it took a new CEO to give voice to the problem and change the habit. Similarly, at Invensys, new CEO Rick Haythornthwaite reported, "Everyone knew the problems, but the structure inhibited them from doing anything about it. People could only take shots across the silos. Some people knew the issues technically and could prevent obviously bad decisions, but they lacked the power to act outside their own fields of concentration. They knew change was needed, but they were not sure how to make it happen."

New CEOs may also have more credibility in representing and respecting customers. In his earliest days at Gillette, Jim Kilts visited a major retailer with a sales executive. Greg Dyke traveled to several BBC studios outside London and immediately endorsed a plan to move them to visible locations in the centers of their cities, where they could connect with audiences more directly. And Haythornthwaite spoke passionately about what he learned from customer interviews. All three understood the powerful, unifying effect of focusing on customers.

Originally published in June 2003
Reprint R0306C

Finding Your Next Core Business

CHRIS ZOOK

Executive Summary

HOW DO YOU KNOW WHEN your core needs to change? And how do you determine what should replace it? From an in-depth study of 25 companies, the author, a strategy consultant, has discovered that it's possible to measure the vitality of a business's core. If it needs reinvention, he says, the best course is to mine hidden assets.

Some of the 25 companies were in deep crisis when they began the process of redefining themselves. But, says Zook, management teams can learn to recognize early signs of erosion. He offers five diagnostic questions with which to evaluate the customers, key sources of differentiation, profit pools, capabilities, and organizational culture of your core business.

The next step is strategic regeneration. In four-fifths of the companies Zook examined, a hidden asset was the centerpiece of the new strategy. He provides a map for identifying the hidden assets in your midst, which tend to fall into three categories: undervalued business platforms, untapped insights into customers, and underexploited capabilities. The Swedish company Dometic, for example, was manufacturing small absorption refrigerators for boats and RVs when it discovered a hidden asset: its understanding of, and access to, customers in the RV market. The company took advantage of a boom in that market to refocus on complete systems for live-in vehicles. The Danish company Novozymes, which produced relatively low-tech commodity enzymes such as those used in detergents, realized that its underutilized biochemical capability in genetic and protein engineering was a hidden asset and successfully refocused on creating bio-engineered specialty enzymes.

Your next core business is not likely to announce itself with fanfare. Use the author's tools to conduct an internal audit of possibilities and pinpoint your new focus.

IT IS A WONDER HOW MANY management teams fail to exploit, or even perceive, the full potential of the basic businesses they are in. Company after company prematurely abandons its core in the pursuit of some hot market or sexy new idea, only to see the error of its ways—often when it's too late to reverse course. Bausch & Lomb is a classic example. Its eagerness to move beyond contact lenses took it into dental products, skin care, and even hearing aids in the 1990s. Today B&L has divested itself of all those businesses at a loss, and is scrambling in the category it once dominated (where Johnson & Johnson now leads). And yet it's also true that no core endures forever. Sticking with an eroding core

for too long, as Polaroid did, can be just as devastating.
Both these companies were once darlings of Wall Street,
each with an intelligent management team and a formerly dominant core. And in a sense, they made the
same mistake: They misjudged the point their core business had reached in its life cycle and whether it was time
to stay focused, expand, or move on.

How do you know when your core needs to change in
some fundamental way? And how do you determine
what the new core should be? These are the questions
that have driven my conversations with senior managers
and the efforts of my research team over the past three
years. What we've discovered is that it is possible to
measure the vitality remaining in a business's core—to
see whether that core is truly exhausted or still has legs.
We've also concluded from an in-depth study of companies that have redefined their cores (including Apple,
IBM, De Beers, PerkinElmer, and 21 others) that there is
a right way to go about reinvention. The surest route is
not to venture far afield but to mine new value close to
home; assets already in hand but peripheral to the core
offer up the richest new cores.

This article discusses both these findings. It identifies
the warning signs that a business is losing its potency
and offers a way to diagnose the strength remaining in
its core. It recounts the efforts of managers in a variety of
settings who saw the writing on the wall and succeeded
in transforming their companies. And, based on these
and other cases, it maps the likely spots in a business
where the makings of a new core might be found.

When It's Time for Deep Strategic Change

Not every company that falls on hard times needs to
rethink its core strategy. On the contrary, declining

performance in what was a thriving business can usually be chalked up to an execution shortfall. But when a strategy does turn out to be exhausted, it's generally for one of three reasons.

The first has to do with *profit pools*—the places along the total value chain of an industry where attractive profits are earned. If your company is targeting a shrinking or shifting profit pool, improving your ability to execute can accomplish only so much. Consider the position of Apple, whose share of the market for personal computers plummeted from 9% in 1995 to less than 3% in 2005. But more to the point, the entire profit pool in PCs steadily contracted during those years. If Apple had not moved its business toward digital music, its prospects might not look very bright. General Dynamics was in a similar situation in the 1990s, when defense spending declined sharply. To avoid being stranded by the receding profit pool, it sold off many of its units and redefined the company around just three core businesses where it held substantial advantages: submarines, electronics, and information systems.

The second reason is *inherently inferior economics.* These often come to light when a new competitor enters the field unburdened by structures and costs that an older company cannot readily shake off. General Motors saw this in competition with Toyota, just as Compaq did with Dell. Other well-known examples include Kmart (vis-à-vis Wal-Mart) and Xerox (vis-à-vis Canon). Occasionally a company sees the clouds gathering and is able to respond effectively. The Port of Singapore Authority (now PSA International), for example, fought off threats from Malaysia and other upstart competitors by slashing costs and identifying new ways to add value for customers. But sometimes the economics are driven by laws or entrenched arrangements that a company cannot change.

The third reason to rethink a core strategy is *a growth formula that cannot be sustained.* A manufacturer of a specialized consumer product—cell phones, say—might find its growth stalling as the market reaches saturation or competitors replicate its once unique source of differentiation. Or a retailer like Home Depot might see its growth slow as competitors like Lowe's catch up. A company that has prospered by simply reproducing its business model may run out of new territory to conquer: Think of the difficulties Wal-Mart has encountered as the cost-benefit ratio of further expansion shifts unfavorably. The core business of a mining company might expire as its mines become depleted. In all such circumstances, finding a new formula for growth depends on finding a new core.

For most of the companies my team and I studied, recognition that the core business had faltered came very late. The optical instruments maker PerkinElmer, the diamond merchant De Beers, the audio equipment manufacturer Harman International—these were all companies in deep crisis when they began their redefinition. Is it inevitable that companies will be blindsided in this way? Or can a management team learn to see early signs that its core strategy is losing relevance?

With that possibility in mind, it would seem reasonable to periodically assess the fundamental vitality of your business. The exhibit "Evaluate Your Core Business" offers a tool for doing so. Its first question looks at the core in terms of the customers it serves. How profitable are they—and how loyal? Arriving at the answers can be difficult, but no undertaking is more worthwhile; strategy goes nowhere unless it begins with the customer.

Evaluate Your Core Business

Five broad questions can help you determine when it is time to redefine your company's core business. For most companies, the answers to these questions can be found by examining the categories listed next to each one.

If the answers reveal that large shifts are about to take place in two or more of these five areas, your company is heading into turbulence; you need to reexamine the fundamentals of your core strategy and even the core itself.

Question	Take a close look at
1. What is the state of our core customers?	· Profitability · Market share · Retention rate · Measures of customer loyalty and advocacy · Share of wallet
2. What is the state of our core differentiation?	· Definition and metrics of differentiation · Relative cost position · Business models of emerging competitors · Increasing or decreasing differentiation
3. What is the state of our industry's profit pools?	· Size, growth, and stability · Share of profit pools captured · Boundaries · Shifts and projections · High costs and prices
4. What is the state of our core capabilities?	· Inventory of key capabilities · Relative importance · Gaps vis-à-vis competitors and vis-à-vis future core needs
5. What is the state of our culture and organization?	· Loyalty and undesired attrition · Capacity and stress points · Alignment and agreement with objectives · Energy and motivation · Bottlenecks to growth

The second question probes your company's key sources of differentiation and asks whether they are strengthening or eroding. The third focuses on your industry's profit pools, a perspective that is often neglected in the quest for revenue and market share growth. Where are the best profits to be found? Who earns them now? How might that change? The fourth examines your company's capabilities—a topic we shall soon turn to—and the fifth assesses your organization's culture and readiness to change.

At the least, managers who go through this exercise tend to spot areas of weakness to be shored up. More dramatically, they may save a business from going under. Note, however, that no scoring system is attached to this diagnostic tool—there is no clearly defined point at which a prescription for strategic redefinition is issued. That would lend false precision to what must be a judgment call by a seasoned management team. The value of the exercise is to ensure that the right questions are taken into account and, by being asked consistently over time, highlight changes that may constitute growing threats to a company's core.

Recognizing the Makings of a New Core

Management teams react in different ways when they reach the conclusion that a core business is under severe threat. Some decide to defend the status quo. Others want to transform their companies all at once through a big merger. Some leap into a hot new market. Such strategies are inordinately risky. (Our analysis suggests that the odds of success are less than one in ten for the first two strategies, and only about one in seven for the third.) The companies we found to be most successful in remaking themselves proceeded in a way that left less to chance. Consider, for example, the transformation of the Swedish company Dometic.

Dometic's roots go back to 1922, when two engineering students named Carl Munters and Baltzar von Platen applied what was known as absorption technology to refrigeration. Whereas most household refrigerators use compressors driven by electric motors to generate cold, their refrigerator had no moving parts and no need for electricity; only a source of heat, as simple as a propane tank, was required. So the absorption refrigerator is particularly useful in places like boats and recreational vehicles, where electric current is hard to come by. In 1925 AB Electrolux acquired the patent rights. The division responsible for absorption refrigerators later became the independent Dometic Group.

By 1973 Dometic was still a small company, with revenues of just 80 million kronor (about U.S. $16.9 million). Worse, it was losing money. Then Sven Stork, an executive charged with fixing the ailing Electrolux product line, began to breathe new life into the business. Stork, who went on to become president and CEO of the company, moved aggressively into the hotel minibar market, where the absorption refrigerator's silent operation had a real advantage over conventional technology. Fueled by those sales, Dometic grew and was able to acquire some of its competitors.

The real breakthrough came when Stork's team focused more closely on the RV market, which was just then beginning to explode. The point wasn't to sell more refrigerators to the RV segment; the company's market share within that segment was already nearly 100%. Rather, it was to add other products to the Dometic line, such as air-conditioning, automated awnings, generators, and systems for cooking, lighting, sanitation, and water purification. As Stork explains, "We decided to make the RV into something that you could really live in. The idea was obvious to people who knew the customers, yet it took a while to convince the manufacturers and especially the rest of our own organization." These moves fundamentally shifted the company's core. Dometic was no longer about absorption refrigeration: It was about RV interior systems and the formidable channel power gained by selling all its products through the same dealers and installers. That channel power allowed Dometic to pull off a move that enhanced its cost structure dramatically. The company streamlined its go-to-market approach in the United States by skipping a distribution layer that had always existed and approaching RV dealers directly. "We prepared for the risks like a military operation," Stork recalls, "and it was a fantastic hit. We were the only company large enough to pull this off. It let us kill off competitors faster than they could come out of the bushes." By 2005 Dometic had grown to KR 7.3 billion, or roughly U.S. $1.2 billion. No longer part of Electrolux (the private equity firm EQT bought it in 2001 and sold it to the investment firm BC Partners a few years later), the company was highly profitable and commanded 75% of the world market share for RV interior systems.

Dometic's story of growth and redefinition is especially instructive because it features all the elements we've seen repeatedly across the successful core-redefining companies we've studied. These are: (1) gradualism during transformation, (2) the discovery and use of hidden assets, (3) underlying leadership economics central to the strategy, and (4) a move from one repeatable formula that is unique to the company to another.

"Gradualism" refers to the fact that Dometic never made anything like a "bet the company" move—often tempting when a business is on the ropes, but almost always a loser's game. As in the other cases of strategic renewal we studied, it redefined its core business by shifting its center of gravity along an existing vector of growth. To do this, it relied on hidden assets—resources or capabilities that it had not yet capitalized on. In Dometic's case, the treasure was its understanding of and access to customers in the RV market.

Leadership economics is a hallmark of almost every great strategy; when we see a situation in which the rich get richer, this is the phenomenon at work. Consider that most industries have more than six competitors, but usually more than 75% of the profit pool is captured by the top two. Of those two, the one with the greatest market power typically captures 70% of total profits and 75% of profits above the cost of capital. When Dometic focused on a defined market where it could stake out a leadership position, enormous financial benefits followed.

Its new growth formula offers the same kind of repeatability the old one did. Recall that Dometic's first focus was on applications for absorption refrigeration, which it pursued product by product, one of which was for RVs. The new formula angled off into a sequence of interior components for the RV customer base. Recently, as RV sales have slowed, Dometic has moved into interior systems for "live-in" vehicles in general, including boats and long-haul trucks.

Where Assets Hide

The importance of a company's overlooked, undervalued, or underutilized assets to its strategic regeneration cannot be overstated. In 21 of the 25 companies we examined, a hidden asset was the centerpiece of the new strategy.

Some of their stories are well known. A few years ago, a struggling Apple realized that its flair for software, user-friendly product design, and imaginative marketing could be applied to more than just computers—in particular, to a little device for listening to music. Today Apple's iPod-based music business accounts for nearly 50% of the company's revenues and 40% of profits—a new core. IBM's Global Services Group was once a tiny services and network-operations unit, not even a stand-alone business within IBM. By 2001 it was larger than all of IBM's hardware business and accounted for roughly two-thirds of the company's market value.

Why would well-established companies even have hidden assets? Shouldn't those assets have been put to work or disposed of long since? Actually, large, complex organizations always acquire more skills, capabilities, and business platforms than they can focus on at any one time. Some are necessarily neglected—and once they have been neglected for a while, a company's leaders often continue to ignore them or discount their value. But then some thing happens: Market conditions change, or perhaps the company acquires new capabilities that complement its forgotten ones. Suddenly the ugly ducklings in the backyard begin to look like swans in training.

The real question, then, is how to open management's eyes to the hidden assets in its midst. One way is to identify the richest hunting grounds. Our research suggests that hidden assets tend to fall into three categories: undervalued business platforms, untapped insights into customers, and underexploited capabilities. The exhibit

"Where Does Your Future Lie?" details the types of assets we've seen exploited in each category. For a better understanding of how these assets came to light, let's look at some individual examples.

UNDERVALUED BUSINESS PLATFORMS

PerkinElmer was once the market leader in optical electronics for analytical instruments, such as spectrophotometers and gas chromatographs. Its optical capabilities were so strong that the company was chosen to manufacture the Hubble Space Telescope's mirrors and sighting equipment for NASA. Yet by 1993 PerkinElmer,

---

Where Does Your Future Lie?

If the core of your business is nearing depletion, the temptation may be great to venture dramatically away from it—to rely on a major acquisition, for instance, in order to establish a foothold in a new, booming industry. But the history of corporate transformation shows you're more likely to be successful if you seek change in your own backyard.

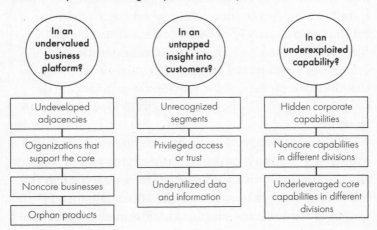

its core product lines under attack by lower-cost and more innovative competitors, had stalled out. Revenues were stuck at $1.2 billion, exactly where they had been ten years earlier, and the market value of the company had eroded along with its earnings; the bottom line showed a loss of $83 million in 1993. In 1995 the board hired a new CEO, Tony White, to renew the company's strategy and performance and, if necessary, to completely redefine its core business.

As White examined the range of product lines and the customer segments served, he noticed a hidden asset that could rescue the company. In the early 1990s, PerkinElmer had branched out in another direction—developing products to amplify DNA—through a strategic alliance with Cetus Corporation. In the process, the company obtained rights to cutting-edge procedures known as polymerase chain reaction technology—a key life-sciences platform. In 1993, the company also acquired a small Silicon Valley life-sciences equipment company, Applied Biosystems (AB)—one more line of instruments to be integrated into PerkinElmer's.

White began to conceive of a redefined core built around analytical instruments for the fast-growing segment of life-sciences labs. The AB instruments in the company's catalog, if reorganized and given appropriate resources and direction, could have greater potential than even the original core. White says, "I was struck by how misconceived it was to tear AB apart and distribute its parts across the functions in the organization. I thought, 'Here is a company whose management does not see what they have.' So one of the first steps I took was to begin to reassemble the parts of AB. I appointed a new president of the division and announced that I was going to re-form the core of the company over a three-year period around this unique platform with leadership in key life-sciences detection technology."

Over the next three years, White and his team separated PerkinElmer's original core business and all the life-sciences products and services into two organizations. The employees in the analytical instruments division were given incentives to meet an aggressive cost reduction and cash flow target and told that the division would be spun off as a separate business or sold to a strong partner. Meanwhile, White set up a new data and diagnostics subsidiary, Celera Genomics, which, fueled by the passion of the scientist Craig Venter, famously went on to sequence the complete human genome. Celera and AB were combined into a new core business organization, a holding company christened Applera.

While Celera garnered the headlines, AB became the gold standard in the sequencing instrument business, with the leading market share. Today it has revenues of $1.9 billion and a healthy net income of $275 million. Meanwhile, the original instrument company was sold to the Massachusetts-based EG&G. (Soon after, EG&G changed its corporate name to PerkinElmer—and has since prospered from a combination that redefined its own core.)

The PerkinElmer-to-Applera transformation offers several lessons. The first is that a hidden asset may be a collection of products and customer relationships in different areas of a company that can be collected to form a new core. The second lesson is the power of market leadership: Finding a subcore of leadership buried in the company and building on it in a focused way created something that started smaller than the original combination but became much bigger and stronger. The third lesson lies in the concept of shrinking to grow. Though it sounds paradoxical and is organizationally difficult for companies to come to grips with, this is one of the most underused and underappreciated growth strategies. (See the sidebar "Shrinking to Grow," at the end of this article.)

Creating a new core based on a previously overlooked business platform is more common than one might think. General Electric, for instance, like IBM, identified an internal business unit—GE Capital—that was undervalued and underutilized. Fueled by new attention and investment, the once sleepy division made more than 170 acquisitions over a ten-year period, propelling GE's growth. By 2005 GE Capital accounted for 35% of the parent corporation's profits. Nestlé discovered that it had a number of food and drink products designed to be consumed outside the home. Like the original PerkinElmer, it assembled these products into a new unit, Nestlé Food Services; developed a unified strategy; and effectively created the core of a new multibillion-dollar business.

UNTAPPED INSIGHTS INTO CUSTOMERS

Most large companies gather considerable amounts of data about the people and businesses that buy their wares. But it's not always clear how much they actually know about those customers. In a recent series of business seminars I held for management teams, the participants took an online survey. Though nearly all came from well-regarded companies, fewer than 25% agreed with the simple statement "We understand our customers." In a 2004 Bain survey, we asked respondents to identify the most important capabilities their companies could acquire to trigger a new wave of growth. "Capabilities to understand our core customers more deeply" topped the list.

For just this reason, insights into and relationships with customers are often hidden assets. A company may discover that one neglected customer segment holds the key to unprecedented growth. It may find that it is in a position of influence over its customers, perhaps because of the trust and reputation it enjoys, and that it has not fully developed this position. Or it may find that it has proprietary data that can be used to alter, deepen, or broaden its customer relationships. All these can stimulate growth around a new core.

Harman International, a maker of high-end audio equipment, redefined its core around an unexploited customer segment. In the early 1990s it was focused primarily on the consumer and professional audio markets, with less than 10% of revenues coming from the original-equipment automotive market. But its growth had stagnated and its profits were near zero. In 1993 Sidney Harman, a cofounder, who had left the company to serve as U.S. deputy secretary of commerce, returned as CEO in an attempt to rejuvenate the company.

Harman cast a curious eye on the automotive segment. He realized that people were spending more time in their cars, and that many drivers were music lovers accustomed to high-end equipment at home. Hoping to beef up the company's sales in this sector, he acquired the German company Becker, which supplied radios to Mercedes-Benz. One day when Harman was visiting their plant, some Becker engineers demonstrated how new digital hardware allowed the company to create high-performance audio equipment in a much smaller space than before. That, Harman says, was the turning point.

He invested heavily in digital to create branded high-end automotive "infotainment" systems. The systems proved to have immense appeal both for car buyers and for car manufacturers, who enjoyed healthy margins on the equipment. Based largely on its success in the automotive market, Harman's market value increased 40-fold from 1993 to 2005.

It is somewhat unusual, of course, to find an untapped customer segment that is poised for such rapid growth. But it isn't at all unusual for a company to discover that its relationships with customers are deeper than it realized, or that it has more knowledge about customers than it has put to work. Hyperion Solutions, a producer of financial software, was able to reinvent itself around new products and a new sales-and-service platform precisely because corporate finance departments had come to depend on its software for financial consolidation and SEC reporting. "We totally underestimated how much they relied upon us for this very technical and sensitive part of their job," says Jeff Rodek, formerly Hyperion's CEO and now the executive chairman. American Express transformed its credit-card business on the basis of previously unutilized knowledge of how different customer segments used the cards and what other products might appeal to them. Even De Beers, long known for its monopolistic practices in the diamond industry, recently redefined its core around consumer and customer relationships. De Beers, of course, had long-standing relationships with everyone in the industry. When its competitive landscape changed with the emergence of new rivals, De Beers leaders Nicky Oppenheimer and Gary Ralfe decided to make the company's strong brand and its unique image and relationships the basis of a major strategic redefinition. The company liquidated 80% of its inventory—the stockpile that had allowed it for so long to stabilize diamond prices—and created a new business model. It built up its brand through advertising. It developed new product ideas for its distributors and jewelers, and sponsored ad campaigns to market them to consumers. As a result, the estimated value of De Beers's diamond business increased nearly tenfold. The company is still in the business of selling rough diamonds, but its core is no longer about controlling supply—it's about serving consumers and customers.

UNDEREXPLOITED CAPABILITIES

Hidden business platforms and hidden customer insights are assets that companies already possess; in theory, all that remains is for management to uncover them and put them to work. Capabilities—the ability to perform specific tasks over and over again—are different. Any capability is potentially available to any company. What matters is how individual companies combine multiple capabilities into "activity systems," as Michael Porter calls them, meaning combinations of business processes that create hard-to-replicate competitive advantage. IKEA's successful business formula, Porter argued in his 1996 HBR article "What Is Strategy?," can be traced to a strong and unique set of linked capabilities, including global sourcing, design for assembly, logistics, and cost management.

An underexploited capability, therefore, can be an engine of growth if and only if it can combine with a company's other capabilities to produce something distinctly new and better. Consider the Danish company Novozymes, now a world leader in the development and production of high-quality enzymes. When it was spun off from its parent corporation in 2000, Novozymes was still largely dependent on relatively low-tech commodity enzymes such as those used in detergents.

Steen Riisgaard, the company's chief executive, set out to change that, and the key was Novozymes's under-utilized scientific capability. Riisgaard focused the company's R&D on the creation of bioengineered specialty enzymes. Its scientists worked closely with customers in order to design the enzymes precisely to their specifications. If a customer wanted to remove grease stains from laundry at unusually low temperatures, for instance, Novozymes would collect possible enzyme-producing microorganisms from all over the world, determine which one produced the enzyme closest to what was needed, remove the relevant gene, and insert the gene into an organism that could safely be produced at high volume. Riisgaard likens the process to finding a needle in a haystack, except that Novozymes uses state-of-the-art technology to single out the haystacks and accelerate the search. Such capabilities have shortened product development from five years to two and have set Novozymes apart from its competitors.

Of course, a company may find that it needs to acquire new capabilities to complement those it already has before it can create a potent activity system. Apple indisputably capitalized on its strengths in design, brand management, user interface, and elegant, easy-to-use software in creating the iPod. But it also needed expertise in the music business and in digital rights management. Once it had those, Apple gained access to content by signing up the top four recording companies before competitors could and developing the iTunes Music Store. It also created a brilliantly functional approach to digital rights management with its Fairplay software, which ensures that the music companies obtain a highly controllable revenue stream. This combination of existing and new capabilities proved transformational for Apple.

The highest form of capability development is to create a unique set of capabilities—no longer hidden—that can build one growth platform after another, repeatedly giving a company competitive advantage in multiple markets. Though difficult, this is a strong temptation; indeed, it has proved to be a siren song for many. But a few companies, such as Emerson Electric, Valspar, Medtronic, and Johnson & Johnson, have managed to avoid the rocks. A lesser-known example is Danaher, which only 20 years ago was a midsize company with $617 million in revenues and almost all its business concentrated in industrial tool markets. Danaher developed a set of procedures whereby it can identify acquisitions and then add value to the acquired companies through the so-called Danaher Business System. The system has several phases and dimensions, including cultural values, productivity improvement, sourcing techniques, and a distinctive approach to measurement and control. It has allowed Danaher to expand into six strategic platforms and 102 subunits spanning a wide range of industrial applications, from electronic testing to environmental services. The company's stock price has risen by more than 5,000% since 1987, outpacing the broader market by a factor of more than five.

It's somewhat maddening how the assets explored here—PerkinElmer's undervalued business platform, Harman's untapped customer insights, Novozymes's underexploited capabilities—can be so obvious in hindsight and yet were so hard to appreciate at the time. Will you be any better able to see what is under your nose? One thing seems clear: Your next core business will not announce itself with fanfare. More likely, you will arrive at it by a painstaking audit of the areas outlined in this article.

The first step is simply to shine a light on the dark corners of your business and identify assets that are candidates for a new core. Once identified, these assets must be assessed. Do they offer the potential of clear, measurable differentiation from your competition? Can they provide tangible added value for your customers? Is there a robust profit pool that they can help you target? Can you acquire the additional capabilities you may need to implement the redefinition? Like the four essentials of a good golf swing, each of these requirements sounds easily met; the difficulty comes in meeting all four at once. Apple's iPod-based redefinition succeeded precisely because the company could answer every question in the affirmative. A negative answer to any one of them would have torpedoed the entire effort.

A Growing Imperative for Management

Learning to perform such assessments and to take gradual, confident steps toward a new core business is increasingly central to the conduct of corporate management. Look, for example, at the fate of the *Fortune* 500 companies in 1994. A research team at Bain found that a decade later 153 of those companies had either gone bankrupt or been acquired, and another 130 had engineered a fundamental shift in their core business strategy. In other words, nearly six out of ten faced serious threats to their survival or independence during the decade, and only about half of this group were able to meet the threat successfully by redefining their core business.

Why do so many companies face the need to transform themselves? Think of the cycle that long-lived companies commonly go through: They prosper first by focusing relentlessly on what they do well, next by expanding on that core to grow, and then, when the core has lost its relevance, by redefining themselves and focusing anew on a different core strength. It seems clear that this focus-expand-redefine cycle has accelerated over the decades. Companies move from one phase to another faster than they once did. The forces behind the acceleration are for the most part well known. New technologies lower costs and shorten product life cycles. New competitors—currently in China and India—shake up whole industries. Capital, innovation, and management talent flow more freely and more quickly around the globe. The churn caused by all this is wide-ranging. The average holding period for a share of common stock has declined from three years in the 1980s to nine months today. The average life span of companies has dropped from 14 years to just over ten, and the average tenure of CEOs has declined from eight years a decade ago to less than five today.

Business leaders are acutely aware of these waves of change and their ramifications. In 2004 my colleagues and I surveyed 259 senior executives around the world about the challenges they faced. More than 80% of them indicated that the productive lives of their strategies were getting shorter. Seventy-two percent believed that their leading competitor would be a different company in five years. Sixty-five percent believed that they would need to restructure the business model that served their primary customers. As the focus-expand-redefine cycle continues to pick up speed, each year will find more companies in that fateful third phase, where redefinition is essential. For most, the right way forward will lie in assets that are hidden from view—in neglected businesses, unused customer insights, and latent capabilities that, once harnessed, can propel new growth.

Shrinking to Grow

WHEN A COMPANY UNCOVERS an underutilized source of leadership economics, sometimes the best response is to "double down" on its investment in that area. A bold version of this is actually shrinking to grow. Consider the example of Royal Vopak.

If you are not in the oil or chemicals business, you may not be familiar with Vopak, but it is the world leader in independent tank storage of bulk oil and chemicals, operating in 75 port locations from Rotterdam to Houston to Singapore. Vopak traces its roots back to a time when the Netherlands was the wealthiest and most powerful country in the world, owing to its role as a center for shipping and trade with the Far East. The origins of Vopak lie in a company that was founded in 1616, by a group of porters on the docks of Amsterdam, for the purpose of loading and unloading ship cargoes.

By 2000 Vopak was enjoying sales of €5.6 billion, with positions in shipping, chemical distribution, and port storage facilities. Its storage business was the most profitable. When Vopak's profits suffered and its stock price came under severe pressure, plummeting from €25 per share in June 1999 to €12 in July 2002, the company took decisive action. It spun off everything but the storage business, reducing the sales volume of the company to €750 million. But Vopak did not stop there: It even sold some of its storage portfolio, further reducing its size.

What was the result? Amazingly, the company's market value increased beyond its original level, as the stock price rebounded to €30 in May 2006. Furthermore, the stronger, well-funded business began to grow again—both organically and through acquisitions and new port locations. During the first half of 2006, Vopak's revenues grew by 17% and its earnings by 28%, in an inherently low-growth industry. John Paul Broeders, the chairman of the executive board, says, "Without shrinking first, we would never have created the resources, the management focus, and a stable platform to begin to grow again as we have."

Shrink-to-grow strategies are not an end in themselves, but they can pave the way for redefinition. These moves have a very high success rate when it comes to increasing a company's value and liberating one of the cores to strengthen and grow, provided it's given additional resources. Indeed, another three of our 25 case studies in successful core redefinition relied on this tactic: PerkinElmer, Samsung, and GUS.

Seven Steps to a New Core Business

1. Define the core of your business. Reach consensus on the true state of the core.

2. Assess the core's full potential and the durability of its key differentiation.

3. Develop a point of view about the future, and define the status quo.

4. Identify the full range of options for redefining the core from the inside and from the outside.

5. Identify your hidden assets, and ask whether they create new options or enable others.

6. Use key criteria (leadership, profit pool, repeatability, chances of implementation) in deciding which assets to employ in redefining your core.

7. Set up a program office to help initiate, track, and manage course corrections.

Originally published in April 2007
Reprint R0704D

Zeitgeist Leadership

ANTHONY J. MAYO AND NITIN NOHRIA

Executive Summary

COMPANIES AND LEADERS DON'T succeed or fail in a vacuum. When it comes to long-term success, the ability to understand and adapt to changing business conditions is at least as important as any particular personality trait or competency.

A clear picture of how powerful the zeitgeist can be emerges from the authors' comprehensive study of the way the business landscape in the United States evolved, decade by decade, throughout the twentieth century. Six contextual factors in particular, they found, most affected the prospects for business: the level of government intervention in business, global events, demographics, shifts in social mores, developments in technology, and the strength or weakness of the labor movement.

A lack of contextual sensitivity can trip up even the most brilliant executive. No less a luminary than

123

Alfred P. Sloan was relieved of GM's day-to-day management in the 1930s because he was unwilling to meet with the new UAW. Conversely, an understanding of the zeitgeist can play a crucial but unheralded role in business performance. Jack Welch is widely credited with GE's remarkable success during the 1980s and 1990s, for example, but far less attention has been paid to his predecessor, the statesmanlike and prudent Reginald Jones, who sustained strong revenue and profit growth during the heavily regulated stagflation of the 1970s.

To better understand this connection between business performance and context, the authors studied 1,000 great U.S. business leaders of the twentieth century and identified three distinct archetypes: *Entrepreneurs,* often ahead of their time, overcame dire challenges to build something new. *Managers* excelled at reading and exploiting the existing zeitgeist to grow their businesses. *Leaders* defied context to identify latent potential in businesses others considered mature, stagnant, or in decline.

In every decade, all three archetypes were vital. It is the ongoing regeneration of this pattern in the business life cycle that ultimately sustains development and progress.

A LEADER'S LONG-TERM SUCCESS isn't derived from sheer force of personality or breadth and depth of skill. Without an ability to read and adapt to changing business conditions, personality and skill are but temporal strengths. An understanding of the zeitgeist and its implications has played a critical but unheralded role in some of the greatest business victories of all time. Jack

Welch is widely credited with GE's remarkable performance during the 1980s and 1990s, for example, but his predecessor, Reginald Jones, made the wise decision to name Welch as his successor despite the fact that the younger manager was considered too inexperienced, too impatient, and too reckless for the job. Though they were polar opposites, each was perfectly attuned to his era.

An accountant by training, the reserved and dispassionate Jones ran the business during the 1970s—a time of simultaneous recession and inflation when he nonetheless managed to sustain strong growth in both revenue and profits. He was well suited to an environment where rational planning and prudent investments were the order of the day. It was also a time of heavy regulation, and Jones's statesmanlike demeanor made him particularly effective in negotiations with government regulators. But Jones recognized that global competition was heating up and the company's future success would hinge on nimbleness and a greater capacity for change and, hence, on a new type of CEO. The boundary-busting Welch—who also read the zeitgeist and saw great change on the horizon— was the ideal person to grow the business during headier times.

A lack of contextual sensitivity can trip up even the most brilliant of executives. No less a luminary than GM's Alfred P. Sloan, whose decisions in the 1920s fundamentally shaped the way large companies are run even today, was relieved of day-to-day management of the business in the 1930s because he was unwilling to meet with the new United Automobile Workers union. Before the 1930s, employees had little if any bargaining power, but they made great gains through the decade, and for the first time in U.S. business history, the ability to negotiate effectively with labor became critical to a manager's success.

Labor's power would wax and wane over the years. Indeed, throughout the twentieth century, the overall business context shifted continually. To greater or lesser degrees, factors such as government regulation, social mores, and global events influenced the opportunities available to industries and leaders. Certain conditions were more favorable to some types of businesses than others. The 1920s were very good to consumer products companies and advertising agencies, for instance, because a nation newly out of war was eager to buy, while the 1940s saw a focus on the heavy machinery needed to fulfill the massive military requirements imposed by World War II. And different types of top executives could succeed depending on the context of both the broader business world and the individual business. The kind of person who might be a superstar in a conservative time like the 1950s, when mature industries prospered, might be a hopeless stick-in the-mud in an era that favored new or emerging industries, such as the 1990s (or India today). A CEO who excels during a period of relative freedom might derail during a time of heavy government intervention, when an ability to navigate rules and manage relationships might prevail over an inventive mind. This is not to say, though, that each era was ideally suited for only one type of executive. In every decade, many forces were at play, affecting the context of individual businesses in different ways and affording different opportunities. The ideal CEO for one company in an era was not necessarily the right person to lead another at the same time. What's more, CEOs and founders played an important role in defining the context in which they lived and worked because they not only seized the opportunities of a specific age but also created opportunities that influenced events.

The notion of zeitgeist might be intangible, but the risks of contextual insensitivity are concrete. If you can't read the business landscape, you risk leading your organization in the wrong direction or choosing the wrong successors. To better understand this connection between business performance and context, we studied 1,000 great U.S. business leaders of the twentieth century—individuals who shaped the way Americans—and people around the globe—live, work, and interact. (For our definition of "great," see the sidebar on our methodology at the end of this article.) We identified exemplars of three distinct leadership archetypes—the *entrepreneur,* the *manager,* and the *leader*—and examined the conditions under which each thrived.

While the ability to seize the zeitgeist—a skill we call "contextual intelligence"—proved universally pivotal to their success, the way each of these various individuals exploited opportunities was very different. Entrepreneurs were uniquely skilled at sensing emerging opportunities or the potential of nascent technologies and through perseverance and determination built successful new enterprises. Managers could spot opportunities to aggressively expand the scale and scope of an established business through disciplined resource allocation and execution. Leaders sensed the potential in moribund businesses and found ways to breathe new life into them. (For a fuller description of each approach, see the sidebar "Three Archetypes of Leadership" at the end of this article.)

We organized our study chronologically, sorting the 1,000 business executives according to the decade in which they founded their company or became CEO.

Decades turned out to be a good proxy for different eras or specific combinations of contextual factors. There is a common understanding, for example, of how the 1950s differed from the 1970s. Once we sorted our leaders in this way, what we found was this: While many contextual factors are at play within any era, six factors—government intervention, global events, demographics, social mores, technology, and labor—are especially influential in shaping the landscape for business. (The relative influence of these factors over the years is shown in the exhibit "The Twentieth-Century Zeitgeist.")

Government Intervention

The extent to which the central government intervenes in business matters determines the degree of autonomy afforded business executives and the level of resources a company needs to cope with potentially complicated regulations.

The 1910s was a time of relatively high government involvement, witnessing a flurry of antitrust activity that included the breakup of Standard Oil and American Tobacco. In this period, the government established the Federal Reserve System, transformed its tariff legislation, expanded tax collection, and enlisted the support and cooperation of business for America's entry into World War I. CEOs and founders in that decade had to understand how to navigate the halls of political power.

But that requirement didn't last long. The 1920s saw a return to laissez-faire governing, as a nation newly out of war wanted freedom and adventure. This was a period in which high-profile antitrust suits against U.S. Steel and Alcoa failed, and both corporate and personal income tax rates were cut. Some manufacturers and their advertisers shamelessly invented and marketed remedies for diseases such as bromodosis (foot odor) and homotosis (a malady brought on by the lack of nice furniture)— practices that today would surely catch the attention of consumer advocates and could well land you in court. Even Prohibition, which was enacted in 1919 to reduce crime and improve urban stability, laid the foundation for many underground illegal businesses.

The freewheeling atmosphere evaporated when the 1929 stock market crash brought on a wave of regulation that transformed many businesses, most notably banking. Among the new laws was the Glass-Steagall Act of 1933, which prohibited any company from engaging in both investment-banking and commercial-banking activities. It prompted Harold Stanley to leave J. P. Morgan and cofound Morgan Stanley, an independent bond house that would carry on the securities-trading business that his former employer was forced to exit. Despite the depressed economy, the firm's very success invited further government intervention into the industry. An example of the leader archetype, Stanley was an outspoken advocate for his company and his industry, and his testimony helped fend off further antitrust activity in the 1940s.

Government controls on business remained strong through the Second World War, as business executives were in many cases forced to support the war effort. Many manager-type CEOs seized this opportunity to dramatically expand their overall businesses through product-line conversions or extensions. As the war ended, the technological achievements it generated were turned to commercial applications, and businesses reestablished a much greater level of autonomy. The 1960s was another era of greater government involvement, as the Kennedy and Johnson administrations enacted legislation focused on equal employment, workplace safety, and consumer rights. Periods of heightened regulatory activity don't always unfold in the same way, though. This time, the government's attempts to control mergers and acquisitions within the same industry spawned the conglomerate business model, as companies attempted to skirt antitrust activity. During the last two decades of the twentieth century, government-mandated deregulation of the airline, banking, and telecommunication industries opened the door to many new competitors, once again changing the landscape for business executives.

Global Events

U.S. business executives were relatively immune to global events (and preferred it that way) through the first half of the twentieth century, with the notable exception of the two world wars and the impact of immigration, which provided a steady supply of cheap labor.

While most companies were happy to revert to the comfort of isolation at the end of both wars, some CEOs saw in the country's leadership position at the close of World War II an opportunity to expand into Europe and beyond. Look at Caterpillar. The CEO at the time, Louis Neumiller, fits our definition of the manager archetype, grasping how the shifting business landscape presented new opportunities for his company, all the while running a smooth operation. He resisted pressure from the military to shift his manufacturing operations entirely from bulldozers to artillery during the war, convincing the government that large-scale earthmoving equipment would also be needed on the battlefields. He built a new plant to make engines for army tanks but kept his main operation focused on tractors and bulldozers. They proved as critical in battle as planes and tanks, essential for constructing landing strips, digging ditches, clearing forests, and so forth.

At the end of the war, Caterpillar received an unexpected leg up in its international expansion efforts as its bright yellow, easily recognizable brand of equipment stayed behind when the U.S. troops came home. Most of that machinery was taken over by local European and Asian governments and businesses, which created a new market for the manufacturer. Caterpillar established dealerships and service centers in these areas for training, maintenance, and—most important—follow-on purchases. At the same time, Neumiller's insistence that the company stick to its core competency meant that after the war Caterpillar was well prepared to fill the growing need for earthmoving equipment at home, providing machines for roadway construction, suburban expansion, and other large-scale development in the 1950s.

Although American social attitudes remained isolationist following the war, the relative stability of the 1950s created opportunities for many large companies to, like Caterpillar, gain in scale by capitalizing on the European recovery and expanding globally. Institutions like the World Bank and the International Monetary Fund created some financial stability, and the cold war kept the global political environment stable, if rigid. Expats enjoyed status in their host countries, perceived as bringing American prosperity and products to the old world. Because the United States controlled such a large portion of the world's GDP, it was a comfortable time for American businesses. But manufacturers were dealt a blow in the 1970s, with the oil crisis and the rise of the

Japanese automobile and electronics industries. Companies were forced to focus more closely on processes and quality even as they searched for alternative forms of fuel. As the century drew to a close, communications technologies made truly global competition a reality, and many businesses were jarred out of their complacency and into an international mind-set. For some businesses, though, the process was painfully slow—it took the recession that followed the 1987 stock market drop, and a loss of both global and domestic market share, to stimulate action.

Demographics

For most of the twentieth century, the U.S. population grew apace, driven by periodic spikes in both domestic family expansion and immigration.

During the population explosion that started in the late 1940s and continued through the early 1960s, families began to spread out, and the first suburbs were born, creating a host of opportunities for new businesses, for those perceptive enough to recognize them. Despite the ongoing population migration, for instance, the accepted wisdom of the time was that shopping centers couldn't survive outside city limits. Edward J. DeBartolo, Sr., a founder in the entrepreneur mold, challenged the theory when he built a 23-store plaza—what today is called a strip mall—in a suburb of his hometown, Youngstown, Ohio, in the late 1940s. Onlookers were skeptical, but it was an almost instant success. Moreover, it wasn't long before his "country" shopping center was joined by medical offices and other service businesses. DeBartolo, who had served in the war evaluating terrain for troop maneuvers and other military actions, put his topography skills to use to grow the business rapidly, flying over the highways and byways of the Midwest to choose his next retail locations. (Sears nimbly followed Americans from farms to cities to suburbs as DeBartolo had done but subsequently failed utterly to catch the migration of economic activity to the exurban Sunbelt in the 1980s and 1990s, leaving Wal-Mart with open territory in which to grow.)

Alonzo G. Decker, Jr., son of one of the founders of Black & Decker, was one leader who took advantage of wartime and postwar demographic shifts to breathe new life into a seemingly mature product. The tool of choice for Rosie the Riveter, the Black & Decker drill proved popular with women on the factory line—so much so that many drills were going home in lunch baskets, and defense contractors had to keep reordering them. At war's end, the company added a consumer products line, an enormously profitable move as the suburban revolution brought with it a new do-it-yourself spirit.

Demographic shifts affect not just the market but the workplace. Over the century, employers had to learn to contend with an ever more diverse employee population, as well as totally new demands for work/family balance. During the 1970s, the face of American business began to change dramatically as, once again, droves of women entered the labor force and businesses became more racially integrated. The growing diversity of the workforce in the 1980s and 1990s reflected the changing mix of immigration. As a result of the huge waves of emigration from Latin America during that period, Hispanics now represent the fastest-growing and largest minority population segment in the United States.

The aging baby boom generation is also adding a new level of complexity and opportunity for businesses,

especially as many individuals choose to forgo early
retirement to pursue a second (or third or fourth) career.
Tapping into this wellspring of knowledge and experience may very well prove to be a competitive advantage
for savvy executives in this new decade.

Social Mores

Of all the contextual factors, social mores are the most
cyclical, and the swings can be dramatic. To manage this
factor, therefore, business executives need to be at their
most adaptable and flexible.

When social mores become more liberal, a host of
business opportunities emerge to fulfill new needs and
desires. This occurred on a large scale in the Roaring
Twenties when, with the burden of war past, people shed
their inhibitions and pursued indulgences at all costs. It
was a time of irrationality, excess, and unprecedented
freedom. The stock market was exploding, business
opportunities seemed limitless, and credit was both
cheap and readily accessible. The fads of the times
reflected the carefree mood: nudist colonies, dance
marathons, flagpole sitting. Having contracted through
the war effort, consumer spending flourished in the
1920s, and business executives were all too ready to provide outlets for the public's desires. The products and
services they introduced—from customizable automo-
biles (no longer just the black Ford Model T) to branded
linens (Cannon towels) to talking movies (Warner Bros.'
The Jazz Singer) to frozen foods (courtesy of Clarence
Birdseye)—were designed to ease the way Americans
lived.

The Depression, which followed, ushered in an almost
complete reversal of social mores—a harkening back to

traditions and conservative values. People passed their time in less whimsical ways: collecting stamps, listening to radio soap operas, and playing board games like Monopoly. Small, affordable luxuries replaced auto-mobiles and other large purchases.

The social freedom of the 1920s reemerged on a much larger scale in the 1960s and 1970s, creating myriad new opportunities—particularly within the fashion, music, and media industries—for those willing to address the changing social conditions.

And in the 1990s, the opportunities for business were virtually limitless: The free flow of capital and the irrational exuberance of a get-rich-quick society fueled a sensibility that made a $10,000 backyard grill seem like as good an idea as a cure for homotosis did in the 1920s.

Technology

Technology has had a strong influence on business exec-utives and the companies they launched and led in every decade of the twentieth century.

The interconnection of the U.S. railways, for example, gave rise in the 1900s to the first large corporations, which could now expand to a national scale. The first national brands began to emerge, as products could be more efficiently delivered across great distances. At the same time, a national advertising industry was born, as newspapers and magazines such as Cyrus Curtis's *Ladies' Home Journal* and *Saturday Evening Post* could reach far-ther afield. Subsequent commercialization of technolo-gies developed during World War II also created an enor-mous set of opportunities for business. The 1940s saw the greatest leaps in productivity of any decade. Almost overnight, under the banner of service to country, companies were transformed from low-volume, inefficient entities into highly efficient, standardized production facilities.

Yet technology's impact was not always immediate or obvious; it often took a visionary business executive to understand and then fulfill the potential of a specific development. In many cases, those individuals were entrepreneurs rather than leaders or managers. But they were not necessarily the same people who could then take a resultant business forward and manage it in a sustainable way. Juan Trippe, for instance, an entrepreneur who pioneered international commercial air travel and turned Pan American World Airways into a powerhouse in the 1920s, undermined the long-term success of his airline with his arrogance and heavy-handed approach to management.

Visa International's Dee Ward Hock, another entrepreneur, was an exception, although he was somewhat disdainful of corporate America and several times in his career found himself out of a job for his failure to play by the rules. While at the National Bank of Commerce, Hock had a vision that the newly emerging digital technology would transform the banking business. Long before that became reality, he imagined paperless and instantaneous transactions, 24 hours a day, seven days a week. He was responsible for the first computerized system for the electronic transfer of data between banks, and he pioneered the international magnetic strip, building bridges between domestic and foreign banking operations. He also persuaded a reluctant Bank of America to cede control over the BankAmericard program to a new independent membership organization, National BankAmericard Incorporated (the international equivalent of which was later renamed Visa), and convinced all 2,700 banks licensed to issue cards to join him. In the end, his tyrannical management style was counterbalanced by great personal charisma and the strength of his technological vision.

Labor

Through much of the twentieth century, the role and influence of labor grew steadily, if in fits and starts. Much like government intervention, the labor movement cycled through periods of progress and retrenchment that were tied to the country's overall levels of economic prosperity and opportunity.

In the first three decades, power was weighted heavily on the side of business, though employees gained some bargaining power during World War I. The business executives of the first decade were driven, opportunistic, and innovative. They built companies that often had a far-reaching impact on the way people lived, but they were, for the most part, less concerned about the way people worked. And during the Red Scare of the 1910s and 1920s—which was fueled by wartime anxieties and the Russian Revolution—unions were viewed as havens for radical foreign-born residents and communists. As such, they were viciously attacked as anti-American.

Labor's first real test and opportunity came in the 1930s, during the Depression. Buttressed by a prolabor government, unions began to win victories such as the first federal minimum wage, despite a double-digit unemployment rate. The strength of the union movement would reach its second apex in the 1950s, in tandem with the public's interest in equal opportunity and improved working conditions. So critical was the ability to deal with unions in the 1960s that Harvard Business School made a labor relations course mandatory for all students.

But the rate of union organization has been on a steady decline since its heyday in the 1950s and early 1960s, as manufacturing sectors have increasingly automated and American industry has moved rapidly into a service-based economy. During the last two decades of the century, almost all new job growth was concentrated in the service sector—and Harvard no longer even teaches the subject. Though relatively few business executives in the twentieth century stood out for their treatment of workers, the ones who did were a breed apart—not just for their concern for employees but for the fact that, in many cases, there was no mandate for it. Instead, they chose to manage this contextual factor before it managed them. Henry Ford caused an uproar when, in 1914, he reduced the workweek and doubled wages, becoming the first employer to give workers a reasonable share of revenues. That was not an altruistic gesture; well before his time, Ford reasoned that a highly motivated workforce would be more productive and that turnover would be drastically reduced. People in the labor movement were actually suspicious of the move, largely because they feared that other organizations would shorten the workweek as well, effectively decreasing hourly workers' pay.

WHAT DOES ALL THIS MEAN for the executives of today? The central lesson we can take from business history is that context matters. The ability to understand the zeitgeist and pursue the unique opportunities it presents for each company is what separates the truly great from the merely competent.

Executives at the beginning of the new millennium face the potential for increased regulation, reticent consumers, constant global uncertainty, and vast demographic changes. The euphoria and delirium of the 1990s have been replaced with caution, pragmatism, and conservatism. Given these challenges, it is tempting to try to find the next iconic CEO—the next Walt Disney, say, or Henry Ford. But that impulse causes us to overlook the role that context played in creating Disney's and Ford's successes. There's no knowing how Disney would have dealt with today's hypermedia environment or whether Ford's steadfast and uncompromising focus on productivity would resonate with today's more empowered labor force. Even Jack Welch would find that the business world has changed since he left GE: Heady growth has given way to recession, a halting recovery, and (despite a probusiness administration) a tighter regulatory climate in the wake of corporate scandals.

So if your organization is seeking to fill a key leadership position, you need to move past a candidate's record of success and understand the contextual environment behind that record—and how that influences the context your company currently faces. Consider global events and impending regulations and the role technology may play in future success. And bear your company's goals in mind. If the business is attempting to maximize growth, a manager may be the best choice for CEO. In times of crisis or decline, a leader may be needed. Boards should refrain from recruiting a celebrity CEO if that person's strengths are not properly aligned with the direction in which the company is going or needs to go. Instead, we can learn from our predecessors the value of appreciating and understanding the conditions that influence the business landscape, which in turn can help us choose the right people for the time.

Our Methodology

EACH OF THE CANDIDATES included in our pool of 1,000 business executives had to have been a founder or CEO of a U.S.-based company for at least five years between 1900 and 2000. As such, any CEO whose tenure began after 1996 was excluded from this survey. (In the earlier decades, when "CEO" was not a common term, we chose to use business historian Richard Tedlow's approach to identifying the key executive by designating as such the primary, or perhaps the sole, individual in a firm who was responsible for setting direction, allocating resources, and monitoring company progress.)

Beyond the five-year tenure requirement, business executives had to have demonstrated at least four consecutive years of top financial performance, or they had to have led a company whose product or service changed the way Americans lived, worked, or interacted with one another in the twentieth century. In view of the lack of easily accessible and complete financial information spanning the entire century (especially before 1925), we used a multitiered financial analysis approach to judging top performance—one or the other of Tobin's Q (that is, the ratio of a company's market to book value); return-on-asset ratios; and market value appreciation.

Though dominated by *Fortune* 100-type company executives, the list endeavors to capture the impact of factors other than company size. As such, it includes people outside the traditional business realm. But from the thousands and thousands of individuals who headed large public and small private enterprises alike during the last 100 years, we have sought to identify only that small fraction that sits at the pinnacle of success—leaders whose legacies have truly stood the test of time.

The process of classifying each of the 1,000 business executives into one of the three archetypes (entrepreneur, manager, or leader) involved a review of data from a number of sources, including historical biographies, company documents, press coverage, and other archival material. In reviewing these materials, we focused specifically on how business executives approached their organization at the beginning of their tenure as founder or CEO. Did they forge something new? Did they derive maximum potential from a defined business opportunity? Or did they transform a business? While we have tried to minimize the inevitable subjectivity of this process, we recognize that the classifications are based on our personal judgment and our interpretation of the available secondary-source information.

A full listing of the 1,000 business leaders in our study can be found on the Web site of the Leadership Initiative of Harvard Business School at www.hbs.edu/leadership.

Three Archetypes of Leadership

THE WORD "LEADER" HAS COME to define business executives in a general way. But when we sought to understand the different types of leadership, it became clear that the same word could be applied to one of three essential executive archetypes.

- **Entrepreneurs** are often ahead of their time, not necessarily bound by the context in which they live. They frequently overcome seemingly insurmountable obstacles and challenges to persevere in finding or launching something new.

- **Managers** are skilled at reading and exploiting the context of their times. Through a deep understanding of the landscape in which they operate, they shape and grow businesses.

- **Leaders** confront change and identify latent potential in businesses that others consider stagnant, mature, declining, or moribund. Where some see failure and demise, this breed of executive sees kernels of possibility and hope.

CERTAIN PERIODS OF THE past century may at first glance seem almost ideally suited for the emergence and dominance of a particular type of executive. For instance, the early part of the century may seem to have been made for the entrepreneur. The 1950s might seem perfect for the organization-man manager.

The tumultuous 1970s might seem ideal for the leader. But we found that all three types coexisted and were pervasive through every decade. In fact, we found that all three archetypes were vital to sustaining the vibrancy of the capitalist system. Entrepreneurs create new businesses, managers grow and optimize them, and leaders transform them at critical inflection points. Time and again, the American capitalist system has borne witness to this business life cycle, and it is the ongoing regeneration of this pattern that ultimately sustains development and progress.

The Twentieth-Century Zeitgeist

GREAT LEADERSHIP IS NOT a singular concept. On the contrary, it is a function of the circumstances in which businesses and their top executives operate. The opportunities available to businesses are deeply influenced by six contextual factors—demographics, technology, social mores, government intervention, labor, and global events—and each comes into play to a varying degree at different times. In the 1930s, for example, the U.S. government took an active interest in business affairs, as the country struggled to recover from the Great Depression. That was a dramatic departure from the 1920s, when a laissez-faire postwar attitude gave businesses free rein to operate as they chose. A break-the-rules type of leader with an inventive mind might have excelled in a start-up during the 1920s but be unable or unwilling to navigate the complex regulations pertaining to a maturing company during the decade that followed. The best leaders can sense the winds of change and adapt with the times.

The accompanying chart shows how these six contextual factors played out in business throughout the twentieth century in the United States. It also illustrates how three different executive archetypes—entrepreneurs, managers, and leaders ("leaders" as an archetype, as opposed to the more generalized term for someone leading an organization)—capitalized on the opportunities of their times. It demonstrates at a high level how context influences business and, in turn, how leaders can influence context.

For a full-color PDF of this chart, please visit hbs.edu/leadership.

The Twentieth-Century Zeitgeist

Decade by Decade

The nation's mood shifted constantly. Entrepreneurs, managers, and leaders each seized the new opportunities—and responded to the corresponding challenges—in different ways.

E *Entrepreneurs* **M** *Managers* **L** *Leaders*

Contextual Influence

The relative influence of each contextual factor shifted from decade to decade. The degree to which each played a part is shown on a scale of one to five by the thickness of the shaded background in each row. The categories correspond to the lines in the graph at right, which indicate how the factors shifted in relation to one another across the decades.

1900s

Growing population; vast market expansion; minimal labor impact; initial government intervention but strong big-business power

E Cyrus Curtis, Curtis Publishing, seizes on increased middle-class purchasing power to publish the Ladies' Home Journal and the Saturday Evening Post.
M Clarence Woolley consolidates the radiator industry into American Radiator.
L Frank Ball uses the expired patent for the Mason Jar to build Ball Corporation.

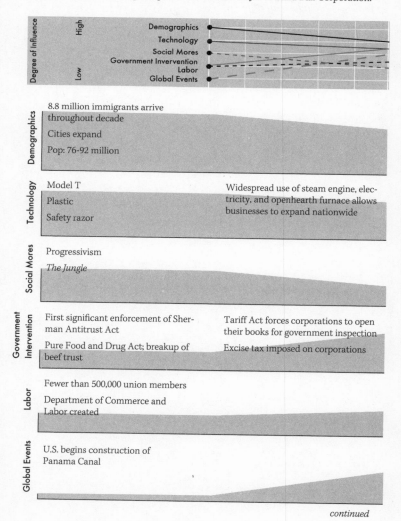

Degree of Influence — High / Low

Demographics
Technology
Social Mores
Government Invervention
Labor
Global Events

Demographics
8.8 million immigrants arrive throughout decade
Cities expand
Pop: 76-92 million

Technology
Model T
Plastic
Safety razor

Widespread use of steam engine, electricity, and openhearth furnace allows businesses to expand nationwide

Social Mores
Progressivism
The Jungle

Government Intervention
First significant enforcement of Sherman Antitrust Act

Tariff Act forces corporations to open their books for government inspection

Pure Food and Drug Act; breakup of beef trust

Excise tax imposed on corporations

Labor
Fewer than 500,000 union members
Department of Commerce and Labor created

Global Events
U.S. begins construction of Panama Canal

continued

1910s

Heavy regulation; business retools for WWI; some small labor power

E Clarence Saunders' self-service Piggly Wiggly stores give consumers access to newly emerging national brands. **M** Frank Phillips cofounds Phillips Petroleum after the breakup of Standard Oil. **L** William Fairburn, Diamond Match, brings new life to the match industry with a nonpoisonous technology.

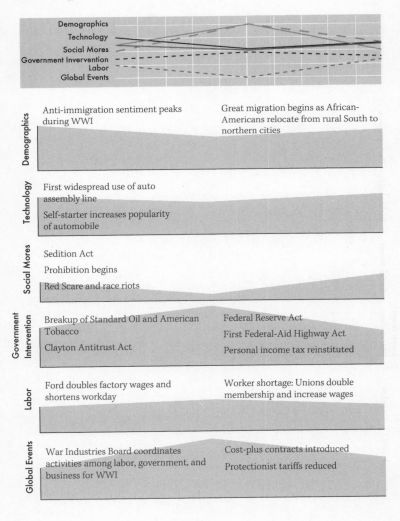

Demographics

Anti-immigration sentiment peaks during WWI

Great migration begins as African-Americans relocate from rural South to northern cities

Technology

First widespread use of auto assembly line

Self-starter increases popularity of automobile

Social Mores

Sedition Act

Prohibition begins

Red Scare and race riots

Government Intervention

Breakup of Standard Oil and American Tobacco

Clayton Antitrust Act

Federal Reserve Act

First Federal-Aid Highway Act

Personal income tax reinstituted

Labor

Ford doubles factory wages and shortens workday

Worker shortage: Unions double membership and increase wages

Global Events

War Industries Board coordinates activities among labor, government, and business for WWI

Cost-plus contracts introduced

Protectionist tariffs reduced

1920s

Government retrenchment; cultural divide between rural and urban residents; broad technology expansion; anti-immigration; massive consumer credit

E Juan Trippe founds Pan Am, the first company to exploit international commercial flight.
M Robert Woodruff makes Coca-Cola a part of Americana with wholesome advertising.
L Gerard Swope revitalizes GE by moving from utilities to consumer products.

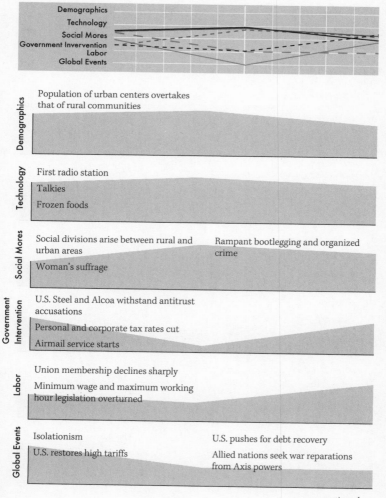

Demographics

Population of urban centers overtakes that of rural communities

Technology

First radio station

Talkies

Frozen foods

Social Mores

Social divisions arise between rural and urban areas

Woman's suffrage

Rampant bootlegging and organized crime

Government Intervention

U.S. Steel and Alcoa withstand antitrust accusations

Personal and corporate tax rates cut

Airmail service starts

Labor

Union membership declines sharply

Minimum wage and maximum working hour legislation overturned

Global Events

Isolationism

U.S. restores high tariffs

U.S. pushes for debt recovery

Allied nations seek war reparations from Axis powers

continued

1930s

Heavy government influence; Great Depression; union progress; technology adaptation; migration

E Margaret Rudkin founds Pepperidge Farm, creating an upscale commodity product. **M** Martin Clement invests in the Penn RR to connect an expanding country. **L** Harold Stanley forms Morgan Stanley to comply with regulations separating commercial and investment banking.

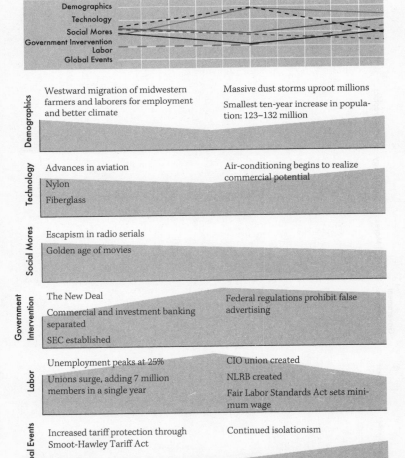

Demographics

Westward migration of midwestern farmers and laborers for employment and better climate

Massive dust storms uproot millions

Smallest ten-year increase in population: 123–132 million

Technology

Advances in aviation

Nylon

Fiberglass

Air-conditioning begins to realize commercial potential

Social Mores

Escapism in radio serials

Golden age of movies

Government Intervention

The New Deal

Commercial and investment banking separated

SEC established

Federal regulations prohibit false advertising

Labor

Unemployment peaks at 25%

Unions surge, adding 7 million members in a single year

CIO union created

NLRB created

Fair Labor Standards Act sets minimum wage

Global Events

Increased tariff protection through Smoot-Hawley Tariff Act

Continued isolationism

1940s

World War II; cooperation among business, labor, and government; postwar baby boom; pent-up consumer demand

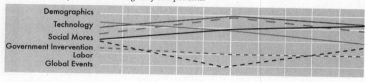 Edward DeBartolo, Sr., develops suburban shopping centers. Louis Neumiller oversees Caterpillar's mobilization for war and later growth in expanding suburbia and abroad. E. Morehead Patterson converts American Machine and Foundry from cigar-rolling equipment to missile systems to bowling-alley components.

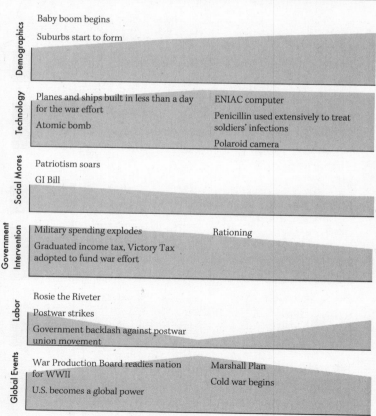

Demographics

Baby boom begins

Suburbs start to form

Technology

Planes and ships built in less than a day for the war effort

Atomic bomb

ENIAC computer

Penicillin used extensively to treat soldiers' infections

Polaroid camera

Social Mores

Patriotism soars

GI Bill

Government Intervention

Military spending explodes

Graduated income tax, Victory Tax adopted to fund war effort

Rationing

Labor

Rosie the Riveter

Postwar strikes

Government backlash against postwar union movement

Global Events

War Production Board readies nation for WWII

U.S. becomes a global power

Marshall Plan

Cold war begins

continued

1950s

Baby boom; business growth unfettered by regulations; conservative social norms; labor progress; technology commercialization; Korean War, cold war

E Ray Kroc masters the franchise operation with McDonald's. **M** Howard Morgens forms P&G Productions to produce TV soap operas. **L** Malcolm McLean, SeaLand Industries, revitalizes the shipping business by creating the containerized cargo system.

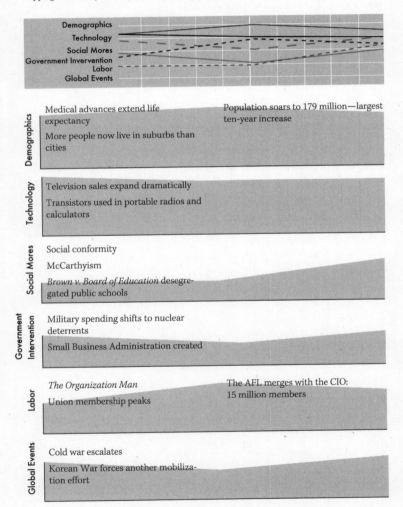

Demographics

Medical advances extend life expectancy

More people now live in suburbs than cities

Population soars to 179 million—largest ten-year increase

Technology

Television sales expand dramatically

Transistors used in portable radios and calculators

Social Mores

Social conformity

McCarthyism

Brown v. Board of Education desegregated public schools

Government Intervention

Military spending shifts to nuclear deterrents

Small Business Administration created

Labor

The Organization Man

Union membership peaks

The AFL merges with the CIO: 15 million members

Global Events

Cold war escalates

Korean War forces another mobilization effort

1960s

Social discord; antitrust legislation; conglomerates; bulging population; space race; booming economy

E Sam Walton refines discount retailing at Wal-Mart. **M** Henry Singleton capitalizes on the conglomerate business model to build Teledyne. **L** Kenneth Iverson, Nucor, uses minimills to revolutionize steelmaking in the United States.

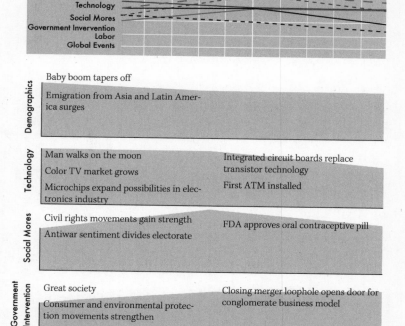

Demographics

Baby boom tapers off

Emigration from Asia and Latin America surges

Technology

Man walks on the moon

Color TV market grows

Microchips expand possibilities in electronics industry

Integrated circuit boards replace transistor technology

First ATM installed

Social Mores

Civil rights movements gain strength

Antiwar sentiment divides electorate

FDA approves oral contraceptive pill

Government Intervention

Great society

Consumer and environmental protection movements strengthen

Closing merger loophole opens door for conglomerate business model

Labor

Factory automation slashes jobs

Civil Rights Act

Equal Pay Act

Unions concentrated in big businesses

Formation of United Farm Workers union

Global Events

Cold war continues to build

Bay of Pigs invasion; Cuban Missile Crisis

Vietnam War escalates

continued

1970s

Oil embargo; stagflation; computer technology commercialized; weakening labor; moderate government intervention; massive international competition

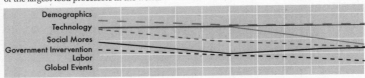 Dee Ward Hock, Visa International, foresees an interconnected world of electronic interchange long before the technology becomes reality. **M** Edmund Pratt, Jr., invests heavily in R&D to make Pfizer a global player. **L** Charles (Mike) Harper transforms struggling ConAgra into one of the largest food processors in the world.

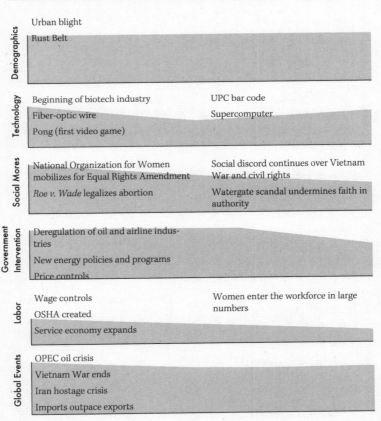

Demographics

Urban blight

Rust Belt

Technology

Beginning of biotech industry

Fiber-optic wire

Pong (first video game)

UPC bar code

Supercomputer

Social Mores

National Organization for Women mobilizes for Equal Rights Amendment

Roe v. Wade legalizes abortion

Social discord continues over Vietnam War and civil rights

Watergate scandal undermines faith in authority

Government Intervention

Deregulation of oil and airline industries

New energy policies and programs

Price controls

Labor

Wage controls

OSHA created

Service economy expands

Women enter the workforce in large numbers

Global Events

OPEC oil crisis

Vietnam War ends

Iran hostage crisis

Imports outpace exports

1980s

Global competition; deregulation; TQM; growing national debt; social conservatism; decline of labor; continued shift to service economy; streamlined business processes

R Reginald Lewis, TLC Group, buys Beatrice Foods in the largest ever leveraged buyout of an off-shore company. **M** Max De Pree restructures Herman Miller with a unique focus on creative design. **L** Lee Iacocca, with massive government assistance, pulls off the turnaround of Chrysler.

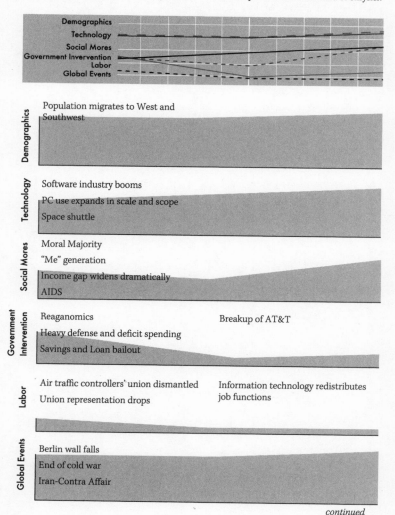

Demographics

Population migrates to West and Southwest

Technology

Software industry booms

PC use expands in scale and scope

Space shuttle

Social Mores

Moral Majority

"Me" generation

Income gap widens dramatically

AIDS

Government Intervention

Reaganomics

Heavy defense and deficit spending

Savings and Loan bailout

Breakup of AT&T

Labor

Air traffic controllers' union dismantled

Union representation drops

Information technology redistributes job functions

Global Events

Berlin wall falls

End of cold war

Iran-Contra Affair

continued

1990s

Globalization; diversity in workforce; reengineering; booming economy; massive immigration; Internet opportunities

E Meg Whitman, eBay, builds the fledgling Internet retail model into a vibrant and passionately loyal community. **M** Alfred Zeien guides Gillette through large-scale product development efforts and targeted acquisitions. **L** Lou Gerstner oversees IBM's turnaround from a manufacturer to a systems integrator and e-business innovator.

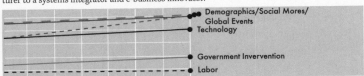

Demographics/Social Mores/
Global Events
Technology

Government Invervention
Labor

Demographics	Immigration tops 9 million (largest number since first decade) Baby boomers age	Hispanics become fastest-growing minority Pop: 250–281 million
Technology	Boom in connectivity Cloning, stem cell research DVDs	
Social Mores	Internet "irrational exuberance" Antigovernment sentiment: Waco standoff; Oklahoma City bombing	
Government Intervention	Family and Medical Leave Act Americans with Disabilities Act Welfare reform	Antitrust action initiated against Microsoft
Labor	Reengineering Record high employment	Service sector outpaces manufacturing in new job creation
Global Events	USSR dismantled; ethnic conflicts exposed Gulf War: real-time TV coverage	Asian financial crisis NAFTA enacted European Union forms

A New Century

How will business leadership emerge in the new millennium? What challenges will we face for the rest of the decade? The last five years have provided some insight into the complexities, challenges, and opportunities for emerging entrepreneurs, managers, and leaders.

Much has changed since the 1990s. Celebrity and hype have been replaced with an emphasis on competence and results. Execution has dethroned vision. And consumer skepticism has overshadowed awe and unfiltered acceptance. In the post-1990s, more attention is being paid to board governance, CEO compensation, reported financial results, and stock option grants. Business schools are reevaluating their curricula, adding new courses on corporate accountability, ethical decision making, law, and board governance.

Not since the scandals of the 1980s have business executives come under so much legal and public scrutiny. Still, Sarbanes-Oxley notwithstanding, the probusiness George W. Bush administration has generally resisted the urge to introduce and enforce greater levels of oversight, leaving it to the business community to self-regulate in many areas and deal with its own mess. Corporations have a short window of opportunity to rise to the occasion. History has shown that if business executives do not take any tangible and meaningful action voluntarily, regulation is likely to snap back with thunderous force and dramatically alter the opportunity structure for business.

While the federal government may be disposed to monitor business somewhat less aggressively than it has in the past, the country has been anything but reticent on the world stage. The war on terror, nuclear proliferation in developing countries, and the festering civil conflicts throughout the Middle East and Africa have heightened the already sensitive and precarious position of the United States in the world. Business executives trying to operate on the global stage must contend with increasing levels of uncertainty and instability. Nevertheless, the long-anticipated opening of the Chinese market might very well provide a new base for American business growth and prosperity.

Computer technology, which was the basis for much of the innovation over the past two decades, will undoubtedly continue to be refined, particularly as advances in wireless communications, data integration, and graphics transfer come to market. Though investments in technology have fallen off precipitously since the Internet implosion, there has been a renewed focus on productive technology—technology with a clear purpose and bottom-line rationale. Technology in the new century will most likely become the domain of managers and leaders rather than entrepreneurs, and their ability to harness its power and capitalize on the latent opportunity of the Internet will set them apart from their peers.

As the baby boom generation moves into its golden years, even greater importance and emphasis will be placed on medical science. Biotechnology, which has yet to deliver on its oft-heralded promises, may be on the cusp of new breakthroughs. Still, the road to discovery will be arduous; social mores have become more conservative, and the new century has already borne witness to contentious debates over research involving stem cells, frozen embryos, and cloning. It may be that, for now, opportunities in this field, too, are best suited to managers and leaders rather than to the entrepreneurs

who have done the initial work, as navigating the contro-
versy will require vision and a deft negotiator's touch.

Labor continues to struggle as companies try to grap-
ple with the recession that followed the collapse of the
Internet bubble and the devastation brought forth in the
wake of September 11. The airline, travel, and hospital-
ity industries have suffered considerably, causing a ripple
effect through a host of other businesses—especially in
the manufacturing sector—that is swelling the ranks of
both multiple-job holders and the underemployed. Outsourcing, which has displaced thousands of jobs, has
become the new strategic mantra for companies attempting to retain or regain their competitiveness on the global
stage. And of course the workplace is facing a dramatic
shift as baby boomers approach retirement age and
companies risk losing vast reserves of knowledge and
experience.

Originally published in October 2005
Reprint R0510B

Cutting Costs Without Drawing Blood

TOM COPELAND

Executive Summary

WHEN LOOKING FOR WAYS TO cut costs, most managers reach for the head-count hatchet, and the markets usually roar with approval. But a company can almost always create far more sustainable value by rigorously evaluating the small-ticket capital items that often get rubber-stamped. Drawing on his experience as a consultant and providing numerous anecdotes, the author contends that those "little" requests often prove to be gold plated or unnecessary.

A disciplined evaluation involves asking only eight questions and conducting postmortems—regular audits of units' capital spending. But the payoff is enormous. Because cutting the capital budget increases cash flow, the author argues that a permanent cut of just 15% in the planned level of capital spending could boost some companies' market capitalization by as much as 30%.

The first three questions—Is this your investment to make? Does it really have to be new? How are our competitors meeting compliance needs?—are asked of operating managers as they assemble capital project requests. The next three are asked by senior managers of themselves and their colleagues as they examine proposals: Is the left hand duplicating investments made by the right? Are trade-offs between profit and capital spending well understood? Are there signs of budget massage? At the end of the review process, senior managers ask: Are we fully using shared assets? How fine-grained are our capacity measures? The author's suggestions for the postmortem include searching for systematic problems with whole classes of expenditures and making sure audit teams come up with specific recommendations for change.

In looking for ways to cut costs—something most companies still need to do despite the good economic times—most managers reach for the head-count hatchet. There's good reason: the markets usually roar with approval. When Eastman Kodak, for example, announced three years ago that it would lay off 10,000 people, saving an annual $400 million in payroll, its market capitalization rose by $2 billion within a few days. Similar stories have played out hundreds of times in the past decade.

But cutting costs doesn't have to be such a bloody process. In my consulting experience over the past 13 years with more than 200 companies in varied industries, I have seen compelling evidence that a company can almost always create far more sustainable value by sensibly reducing its capital expenditures. How? Not by postponing or eliminating big spending projects, which are usually less than 20% of the budget anyway, but by conducting a rigorous, disciplined evaluation of the small-ticket items that usually get rubber-stamped. Those "little" requests often prove to be unnecessary—in some cases they duplicate other requests—or gold plated. But few managers have the time, energy, or inclination to ask about them. They should.

A solid evaluation of small-ticket capital budget items is straightforward. It involves a series of only eight questions, and the payoff is enormous. Cutting the capital budget increases cash flow dramatically, which can have an enormous impact on a company's value in the marketplace. In fact, according to my research, a permanent 15% cut in the planned level of capital spending could boost some companies' market capitalizations by as much as 30%. Better still, the company gets to keep the heads—make that brains—that might have been fired. Paying more attention to small items in the capital budget creates that business rarity—a win-win situation. (For more on the advantages of cutting capital spending, see the table "Capex Dollars Versus Job Dollars.")

But the eight questions don't get asked all at once. They should come in three distinct phases:

- Put the first three to your operating managers as they assemble their capital project requests. The questions will help them submit airtight proposals.

- Put the next three to yourself and your colleagues as you examine the small-ticket proposals. The questions will help you root out much of the gold plating and redundancy built into budget requests.

- Pose the last two questions at the end of the process. They will help you improve it for the next time.

Capex Dollars Versus Job Dollars

You get more bang for the buck—or perhaps more buck for the bang—cutting capex dollars than by cutting payroll. According to my estimates, the increased market valuation that resulted from Kodak's $400 million payroll cuts could have been achieved by a $280 million reduction in capital spending. The reason for the difference, of course, is that a company has to make severance payments—$600 million in Kodak's case—to people it has laid off. (There is no severance pay for capital.) The table compares recent payroll savings at Kodak and several other corporations with my estimated value-equivalent capex cuts.

	Kodak	Hasbro	Whirlpool	Motorola	Nike	Goodyear	DuPont
Date	Sept. 1997	Dec. 1997	Dec. 1997	June 1998	July 1998	April 1999	June 1999
Layoffs (People)	10,000	2,500	4,700	14,000	1,600	2,600	1,400
Savings Per Year from Layoffs, in Millions	$400	$50	$162	$840	$300	$100	$90
Value-Equivalent Annual Capex Cut, in Millions	$280	$30	$105	$538	$68	$72	$69
Capex Cut as Percentage of Total Capex	$14.5%	20.6%	23.7%	22.5%	15.1%	10.3%	3.1%

Source: Compustat, Wall Street Journal, Monitor Group analysis

In the following pages, we'll look in detail at each phase and its questions. None of the questions, to be sure, will sound wildly unfamiliar. But when did you last go to the trouble of asking such questions about a decision involving less than $5 million? The answer may be "Never," which likely means you've been spending more than you should have.

Why Small Requests Go Wrong

Before we look at the questions, it's useful to understand why small-item budget requests are often such a source of waste. The root of the problem is that senior managers with very limited time at their disposal usually feel they can best serve the company by focusing on big-ticket investments. That's not to say that focusing on big-ticket items is wrong—those investments often have huge strategic importance—but one result is that senior managers end up rubber-stamping the small proposals that often make up the remaining 80% of the capital budget.

Rubber-stamping, however, causes problems because the people preparing small-item capital spending proposals typically lack the experience or knowledge to think them through properly. And for a variety of reasons, unit managers will almost inevitably ask for more money than they need. Those reasons can be all too human. Many of the people who generate small-item spending requests are engineers. With the best intentions, engineers often indulge in gold plating. That's a natural by-product of their sensibilities—engineers generally value reliability, redundancy, and technical bells and whistles. Given a choice, they will include top-of-the-line supplies and equipment in their projects.

But it's not just engineers. Anyone at a middle or low level in an organization is likely to be risk averse, which causes overspending. No frontline manager wants to be blamed for having ordered too few spare parts when a crucial piece of machinery breaks down and creates a product shortage. Overspending may also result from unit managers' attempts to protect their turf—a low budget request this year may lead to the unit being short-changed the next.

Finally, a lot of overspending on small items is the result of a perfectly understandable dynamic. Managers on the front line have a natural tendency—even a duty—to focus on their own units' needs rather than on whether their requests overlap with those of other units. And as we'll see, some duplication may be a consequence of processes and measures put in place by senior managers. In such cases, senior managers who fail to keep an eye on small-item capital spending have only themselves to blame.

Let's turn to what senior managers can do to root out the waste—the eight questions they can ask during the budgeting cycle. First, let's examine the three questions that can help get the budget process off to a better start. (For a visual explanation of the questions, see the exhibit "Bringing Discipline to Capital Budgets at AnyCorp.")

Requesting the Right Information

As all Bostonians know, there's no one right way to make New England clam chowder. But whatever the details of the recipe, cooks will always need clams, milk, and potatoes. It's much the same with capital spending. There are three questions that should always be part of the mix when unit managers are cooking up a proposal:

Bringing Discipline to Capital Budgets at AnyCorp

Eight questions and a postmortem can help senior executives conduct a solid evaluation of small-ticket capital budget items. Cutting the capital budget increases cash flow, which can have a huge impact on a company's value in the marketplace.

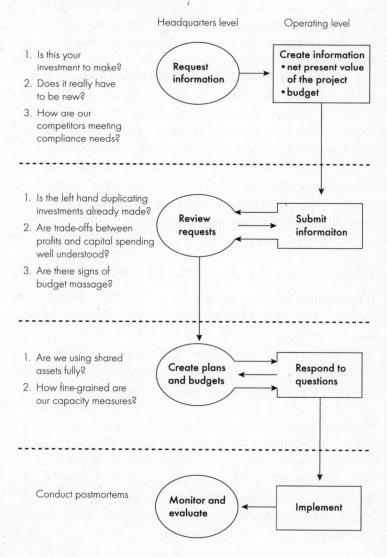

Headquarters level   Operating level

1. Is this your investment to make?
2. Does it really have to be new?
3. How are our competitors meeting compliance needs?

Request information → **Create information**
• net present value of the project
• budget

1. Is the left hand duplicating investments already made?
2. Are trade-offs between profits and capital spending well understood?
3. Are there signs of budget massage?

Review requests → **Submit informaiton**

1. Are we using shared assets fully?
2. How fine-grained are our capacity measures?

Create plans and budgets ← **Respond to questions**

Conduct postmortems

Monitor and evaluate ← **Implement**

IS THIS YOUR INVESTMENT TO MAKE?

Sometimes a unit manager will overstep the boundaries of his control and put in a request for an investment that is the responsibility of someone else in the company—or even of some other organization altogether. That happened at one manufacturer: the sales and marketing group had requested money to buy shares in the company's dealers. The dealers, according to the sales and marketing people, would use the capital to upgrade their facilities and infrastructure. "If you must assist your dealers in upgrading their facilities," I said to the company's managers, "why not provide a financing program for them instead? After all, the storefronts are theirs, not yours." By forcing unit managers to explain why they, rather than others, need to make particular investments, senior managers can head off a lot of unnecessary spending.

DOES IT REALLY HAVE TO BE NEW?

If they could afford it, most people would like to drive a new car. Managers are no different. They instinctively justify buying new machines on the grounds that the old ones need a lot of maintenance. But in my experience, that argument is deeply flawed. Equipment manufacturers in one industry I've studied, for example, routinely spend millions of dollars on new machines years earlier than they need to. In most cases, the overall cost (including the cost of breakdowns) is 30% to 40% lower if a company continues servicing an existing machine for five more years instead of buying a new one. In order to fight impulsive acquisitions of new machinery, companies should require unit managers to run the numbers on all alternative investment options open to them—including maintaining the existing assets or buying used ones. Time after time, managers will go no further than an analysis of the economics of purchasing the new machine. But even if those economics are sound, there's usually a cheaper alternative to buying new.

HOW ARE OUR COMPETITORS MEETING COMPLIANCE NEEDS?

Managers who must make investments to comply with environmental, health, and safety regulations tend to be afraid they'll be blamed for underspending if something goes wrong. This sometimes irrational fear prevents them from thinking as clearly or imaginatively as they should about how to save money on compliance, so they gold plate their investment requests. But a company should plan such expenses with the same rigor it brings to its tax obligations. A good way to combat conservative and costly compliance is to require unit managers to compare their proposals with the practices of other companies.

Reviewing the Budget Proposals

Although senior managers can avoid a lot of mis-spending by getting people to submit the right kind of proposals, some padding invariably gets through. Asking the following three questions during the proposal review helps uncover the fat:

IS THE LEFT HAND DUPLICATING INVESTMENTS ALREADY MADE BY THE RIGHT?

Banks, telephone companies, and other big, far-flung organizations with complicated operations have a tendency to accumulate excess capacity. That's because many different groups of people are involved in the planning and implementation of capital expenditures. The scale of the problem can be impressive. A certain network company, for example, discovered in the course of a spending review that it had inadvertently created a 70% excess capacity in its server network. The company's field engineers, unaware that the people designing the network had built in a 30% extra server capacity, installed so many additional servers to ensure availability that excess capacity was more than doubled. In order to expose this kind of unnecessary spending, managers need to check how well the various decision-makers involved with a particular item are communicating with one another as they pass the item down the line. If there's no regular, honest exchange of information, there's a high chance the company is spending a lot on unnecessary capacity.

ARE THE TRADE-OFFS BETWEEN PROFITS AND CAPITAL SPENDING WELL UNDERSTOOD?

In some companies, no amount of prior consideration will stop managers from sending in requests for new assets. In such cases, it usually turns out that the company suffers from a financial culture that places earnings above all other performance measures. Take the example of a certain telecommunications company. Its network designers insisted on using extra thick telegraph poles and specified that they be placed five feet closer together than required by law. Such a distribution system, they declared, would be better able to withstand falling tree limbs during storms. Asked why the company didn't trim the trees instead, the engineers replied that the cost of trimming would reduce the company's profitability, while the extra capital investment would not, since it wouldn't appear in the earnings statement! Our analysis, which capitalized the after-tax cost of the extra annual maintenance so that it could be compared with the capital cost of the distribution system, showed that the stronger distribution system was several times more expensive.

ARE THERE SIGNS OF BUDGET MASSAGE?

Budget massaging is common at large companies where senior managers don't police capital spending beyond looking to see whether a unit's spending matches its forecasts. In such companies, unit managers may be reluctant to propose reductions in their capital spending because they are afraid the head office won't be generous when they need an increase; on the other hand, they may be afraid that asking for too much money will provoke a close encounter with the company's internal auditors. So they may attempt to massage the budget in a couple of ways. One is to shuffle expenditures between capital and annual operating budgets so that the capital budget never shows a dramatic change from year to year. Another is to practice year-end loading—when managers realize they're going to underspend the allocations they've requested, they start putting in unnecessary expenses to make up the shortfall. A dented fender, for example, becomes an excuse to request a new pickup truck. By going to the trouble during the year to query unit managers about small decisions of this sort, senior managers can discourage units from massaging their budgets.

Revisit Business Processes

After the unit managers have gone off to spend their money, senior managers should look again at the procedures that have been set up to improve the efficiency of the company's spending and make sure they are working. The next two questions can uncover many problems:

ARE WE USING SHARED ASSETS FULLY?

At networked businesses that use a lot of shared assets—car-rental companies, airlines, electric utilities, telecoms, Internet service providers, and the like—spending is highly sensitive to slow-moving bureaucratic procedures. A certain telecommunications company, for example, was investing millions in new servers, even though its network wasn't growing quickly enough to justify the new equipment. The reason, it turned out, was that the official procedure for disconnecting and relocating unneeded servers took so long that they didn't show up as excess on capacity lists until the year after they were deemed unnecessary. The best way for a senior manager to find out if this sort of thing is going on is to check the extent to which shared assets are really being utilized— and not just by looking at extra-capacity lists. If shared assets are not fully utilized most of the time, it's likely you will have to revisit your company's paper trails.

HOW FINE-GRAINED ARE OUR CAPACITY MEASURES?

Not all bureaucracy-induced overspending is a result of slow procedures. Sometimes, overspending is a direct consequence of a company's measures for recognizing that it needs more investment in equipment. If such measures aren't adequately fine-grained, managers can underestimate the capacity of equipment or networks. This happened at a cable company whose capacity measures indicated that a bundle of optical fibers was being fully used if just one fiber was carrying information. But each bundle consisted of 11 fibers; since there were three bundles per cable, a line with 33 fibers could be classified as fully utilized if as few as three fibers were lit. Naturally, the company installed far more cable than it needed.

Conducting a Postmortem

When all is said and done, even the most careful budgeting process is fallible. What's more, in a fast-paced marketplace like the Internet you can lose out by taking time to probe deeply as you make decisions on capital spending. That's why managers need to supplement budget supervision with regular audits of units' capital spending. There are three rules to follow in conducting such inquiries:

BE INCLUSIVE

Many companies leave their audits to people in the finance department, who often confront workers in an adversarial manner. That's wrong. Audit teams should always include employees from the departments being reviewed. For a company to unearth the kind of overspending I've been talking about, it's essential that the people who know most about the operations buy into the process. At the same time, the team needs to have some organizational authority. It is, after all, going to be asking embarrassing questions. The team should therefore report to a senior executive who has the muscle to clear obstacles from its path and make any changes it may recommend.

HAVE A CLEAR GOAL

The audit team should not only identify what went wrong with last year's budget, it should come up with recommendations for change. A good audit should specify ways to save at least 10% of a unit's capital budget. If senior managers want to stretch a team, however, they should set a higher goal of 15% or 20%.

GROUP SMALL ITEMS TOGETHER

The really big savings come when senior managers discover systematic problems with whole classes of expenditures. It's easier to find such problems if you look at all the requests for particular items—transformers at an electric utility or clamps on a pipeline, for example—at the same time. I remember an executive of a chemical company—he was blind—who had his staff construct a detailed scale model of a new chemical plant; having reviewed the design in three dimensions, he reduced the cost of the plant 10% by rerouting pipes to save on expensive elbow joints.

A GOOD AUDIT CAN TURN UP surprising horrors. One of my favorite stories is about a telecommunications company I was advising eight years ago. In the course of reviewing the company's capital spending, I came across an internal rule specifying that all cables be laid at a depth of two meters. I asked the head of engineering about it, and he said that at two meters, the cable network would be protected against a thermonuclear magnetic impulse created by the explosion of a hydrogen bomb. "Fair enough," I replied, "but what happens to your customers when the bomb goes off?" The company saved $80 million a year by reducing its cable depth to one meter. If you make the eight questions and an audit a part of your company's small-item capital budgeting process, you may well find a lot of buried treasure.

Originally published in September–October 2000
Reprint R00503

Leading Through Rough Times

An Interview with Novell's Eric Schmidt

BRONWYN FRYER

Executive Summary

FEW LARGE COMPANIES HAVE soared as high, sunk as low, and struggled as long as the 18-year-old networking software maker Novell. For years, the company dominated the market for local area networks, but by 1997, it had faltered due to misguided acquisitions, product missteps, and large unsold inventories. That's when Eric Schmidt arrived from Sun Microsystems to take over as Novell's third CEO.

He turned the company around with a deft combination of cost reductions, divestitures, and new product rollouts, and by 1998, it was back in the black. Unfortunately, the good times didn't last, and like most technology companies, Novell is once again struggling with a slowdown in demand.

But Schmidt is optimistic about returning Novell to good health, and his strategies suggest ways for other

organizations to handle themselves during downturns.
He counsels against being overly cautious during such
times. It may be necessary to eliminate excess inventory,
cut costs, and reduce the size of the staff and the management team in order to stabilize a company. Working
to retain those employees whom he calls the "smart people" and keeping them motivated will have long-term
payoffs.

Further, Schmidt says it is necessary to acknowledge
and overcome a "culture of fear," the deadening environment of cynicism in which employees suppress thoughts
and feelings because they're worried about layoffs. His
additional advice: keep new products coming out to sustain the interest of customers and the press, pay attention
to your cash position, stay focused on your desired outcomes, and take heart from other industry leaders.

---

*Few large companies have soared as high, sunk as low,
and struggled as long as the 18-year-old networking software maker Novell. Not long after it was founded in
Provo, Utah, in 1983, the company came to dominate
the market for local area networks. But after several misguided acquisitions and product missteps in the mid-
1990s, Novell seemed to be down for the count in April
1997. That's when Eric Schmidt, the highly respected
CTO at Sun Microsystems, surprised the business world
by accepting an offer to become the beleaguered company's third CEO as well as its chairman. His mandate:
put Novell back onto a sound financial footing, refocus it
on its core engineering strengths, and turn it into a leading player in Internet software and network services.*

*The situation Schmidt faced was daunting, to say the
least. Microsoft, with its Windows NT operating system,*

was competing aggressively for the networking market. Novell was saddled with an outdated product line and large unsold inventories. Customers were getting nervous, and reporters were beginning to write the company's obituary. With a deft combination of cost reductions, divestitures, and new product rollouts, Schmidt turned the company around. By 1998, it was back in the black. But the good times didn't last long. Like most technology companies, Novell is now struggling with a slowdown in demand. And in March, the company announced its intentions to acquire Cambridge Technology Partners and to appoint Jack Messman, current CEO of CTP, as CEO of Novell. Now acting as Novell's chief strategist, Schmidt is back in turnaround mode.

It's a mode that seems to suit him. In February, when he sat down in Novell's executive offices in San Jose, California, for this interview, he talked expansively about the challenges involved in bringing a once proud company back to life and then leading it through yet another tough stretch. When you enter a downturn, he said, you have to fight the instinct to be overly cautious. Rather, you have to encourage your most creative people to take chances, to follow their hunches. The alternative is to succumb to a "culture of fear," in which a bleak vision of the future becomes a self-fulfilling prophecy.

In today's unpredictable business world, with its ever shifting markets and competitors, the prospect of a sudden downturn haunts every executive. Eric Schmidt's experience provides more than a cautionary tale; it suggests a path through the wilderness.

A lot of people were stunned when you left Sun for Novell in 1997. Why did you make the move? And what did you find when you arrived?

I had spent a long time—14 years—in a variety of executive positions at Sun, and I'd hit the top of my game as CTO. I was ready to try something new. Over time, I'd become fascinated by network technology, and Novell looked like a good fit with my interests. When I agreed to take the job, I'd done my homework. McKinsey had performed an audit and reported that the company had lots of cash. Novell's main product, NetWare, was a solid brand. I knew that I was coming to an organization that needed help, but I certainly didn't think it was hopeless.

Things were considerably worse than I expected. On my first day on the job, the president told me that it looked like our revenues would be up $20 million for the quarter. That was terrific news. But on day three, he caught me in the hallway. He was ashen. "We have a problem," he said. "Remember what I told you about being up $20 million? Well, it turns out we're actually down $20 million." Our sales were tanking, and we had a lot of inventory backed up in the channel. It was a shock, to say the least.

A few days later, I found myself on a plane sitting next to Roel Pieper, the former CEO of Tandem Computers, which had recently been acquired by Compaq. I told Roel about my problem. He smiled at me and said, "Congratulations. You're about to do a turnaround."

"Are you kidding?" I said. "That's not at all what I signed up for."

"Nonetheless, that's what you're going to do," Roel informed me. "And I can help you. First, you do a big layoff."

"But I didn't come here to fire people."

"Second, you get rid of 80% of your executives."

"You've got to be kidding."

"And," he said, "you do all this in the next three weeks."

"I can't possibly terminate people I haven't met yet," I said. And then I asked myself, "What on earth have I gotten into?"

In my third week on the job, we had to decide what to tell Wall Street regarding our revenue loss. The CFO told me that we had enough revenue reserves, despite high inventory in the distribution channel, to avoid pre-announcing the shortfall. But that strategy made me nervous. I knew that a lot of software companies had run into trouble with the SEC for questionable accounting tricks. I called the cochairman, John Young (the former CEO of Hewlett-Packard), to seek his advice, and he asked me, "What does your gut say?" I said that I felt we should be honest and announce the shortfall. And John said, "I approve." Later, he told me that he knew then that he'd made the right decision in hiring me. But after that announcement, everyone really thought the company was dead as a doornail.

After you got over the shock, how did you go about bringing Novell back to life?

First, of course, you have to stop the bleeding and stabilize the patient. And that requires exactly the kind of tough, fast action Roel Pieper had described. We had what I call a "kitchen sink" quarter, when you clean up the mess. We drained the excess inventory from the channel and cut costs drastically. We laid off more than 1,000 employees and replaced most of the executive management team, reducing seven layers of management to four. Those were painful steps, but they were necessary to save the company. At the same time, I met personally with our major customers to show them what we were doing and to convince them that we were still alive. And we launched an aggressive PR campaign, announcing new products or product upgrades every month. The trade press is crucial in our business, and we had to get the word out that we were moving forward.

While we were making these kinds of tactical moves, we were also repositioning the company strategically and refocusing on our core networking strengths. But neither the cost cutting nor the repositioning represented the biggest challenge we faced when I joined Novell. The biggest challenge was retaining our key talent—the ones I call the "smart people"—and keeping them motivated. A company can survive losing a lot of people, but if it loses its smart people, it's done for.

Keeping your most talented employees must have been particularly difficult given the company's precarious condition. What did you do?

The first thing I had to do was identify them. In a company like ours that is driven by innovation, you can't just look at an org chart to find your most important employees. The key people here are our most creative engineers—they're the smart people, the ones who control our future—and they can be very well hidden in the organization. They're not necessarily at the top of any hierarchy.

I used a kind of algorithm to locate these people. A few days after I started, I was on the company shuttle from San Jose to Provo, where our engineering staff is centered, and I was sitting knee-to-knee with two engineers embroiled in a fascinating, heated argument. They were obviously two extremely bright people. I asked them to give me the names of the smartest people they knew in the company. They gave me a list, and over the next week I set up half-hour meetings with all of those other smart people, and I asked each of them to give me the names of the ten smartest people they knew. Because the smart people in an organization tend to know one another, I eventually found out who they were—about 100 in all.

I met and talked with each of them. It helped that, as an engineer myself, I understood their intellectual and technological needs and what their concerns were. I listened intently while they told me about their experiences and their frustrations. They were very demoralized; no one had listened to them for a long time, and they had basically decided to lie low and keep their mouths shut. As a result, lots of great ideas were being lost.

The more conversations I had, the more clear it became that Novell had a dysfunctional culture, a sick culture. Doctors will tell you that when you're sick, having a diagnosis allows you to focus your energy on overcoming your disease. So my management team worked together to name Novell's condition, and we ended up calling it the "culture of fear." In a culture of fear, which I think is a common condition in companies going through rough times, people are always worried about getting laid off, and so they suppress their feelings. Instead of complaining to their bosses, whom they fear might fire them, they complain vociferously to their peers. That's what was going on here. This situation created a kind of pervasive bellyaching, a corporate cynicism. A related condition, which we came to call the "Novell nod," was ubiquitous. People would sit in a room, listening to someone talk and nodding in agreement. Then, as they left the room, they'd all say to one another, "That was the stupidest thing I've ever heard." I'd see that kind of behavior constantly.

So exactly how do you overcome a culture of fear?

You begin by recognizing that you can't change a culture
by fiat. The problem lies deep within the organization,
and you have to give everyone—not just the smart people—permission to correct it. In our case, that meant
encouraging people to say what was really on their
minds. I remember one instance of this, in a meeting
with a group of engineers. There was something wrong
with the meeting's atmosphere: it was a little too controlled, a little too formal. I kept asking questions, push-
ing for an answer. And finally, one of the engineers
exploded, saying, "I can't take this!" We were all a little
shocked. Then he looked at me and said, "Do I have permission to be passionate?" I said, "Yes, of course!" Then
he stood up and gave this incredibly lucid proposal for a
new product. He'd been so constrained by the culture
that he'd been afraid to promote his idea for fear of being
shot down by his boss.

I spent a lot of time trying to get people to open up in
this way, to give voice to the ideas they'd buried inside
themselves. Some of these ideas were brilliant, and I
encouraged people to work on them. You know, it's a
natural reaction to turn cautious when your company's
in trouble, but that's precisely the wrong tack to take.
You have to give people freedom to pursue their pas-
sions. That's the only way to keep them focused and
inspired and to ensure you'll have a flow of new products
to regain, retain, or grow ground in the market. The new
version of our flagship product, NetWare 5.0, emerged in
this way. After we released it in September 1998, our revenues improved nicely, leading to after-tax profits of
$192 million on revenues of $1.3 billion in 1999. This
built on improvement from the preceding fiscal year

when our after-tax profits were $102 million on revenues of $1.1 billion, compared with a loss of $78 million on $1 billion of revenue in 1997. The turnaround wouldn't have been so dramatic if we'd told people to be careful.

Another way to overcome a culture of fear is to show employees that you understand what the cultural problems are and that you are committed to fixing them. Sales meetings, for example, offer opportunities not only to motivate people and get them excited about new products or directions but also to address cultural issues on a broad scale. At one meeting, I told the audience that we had discovered a secret weapon deep in the bowels of Provo. And I introduced this engineer in a Hawaiian shirt named Ron Tanner. Ron launched into a very funny story about how the management in California has never understood anything and how a few engineers in Utah pulled together as a team and developed this brilliant product for customers. Everything he said resonated with the audience, who were laughing and shouting, "Yeah!" Then he unveiled the product, ZENworks, the first new product developed under my leadership. This product had long been suppressed within the culture of fear, but Ron and his team succeeded in bringing it out. ZENworks now produces more than $100 million in revenues for us. That sales meeting was a wonderful public acknowledgment that there had been suppression—a kind of denial about things like the friction between the Utah people and the California people—but that now the era of suppression was over.

I'm not saying we're completely cured, by the way. The cultural issues have been extremely difficult to eradicate. In fact, I'm less satisfied about this today than I was two years ago. When I first arrived here, I experienced an incredible outpouring of goodwill, as if I'd ridden in on a white horse. But cultural problems are like cancer. They keep coming back. So I still feel the remnants of the culture of fear, and I still sometimes see the Novell nod. The good news is that these problems don't appear in gross forms the way they used to, and, when they do appear, we know how to address them.

Despite the cultural problems, you've had good luck in keeping employees from jumping ship. Novell's turnover rate in 1998–99 hovered around 15%, which was significantly lower than the industry average of 22%. How have you kept people, particularly the smart people, from leaving?

A lot of it is Management 101: repeating the same message 20 times, training the trainers, getting in front of people, cheering them on. We're also fortunate to have our engineering headquarters in Utah, where the competition for talent is much less fierce than in Silicon Valley. We do whatever it takes to hang on to our top talent. Sometimes that includes counteroffers. Most people will tell you that's a bad idea, because extending a counteroffer leads to bidding wars. But when you lose a talented marketing person to the competition, it's a huge cost to your business because great knowledge and skills go to a competitor. Usually, when we ask people why they're leaving, they talk about money. But most of the time, it's something else, like a project or a manager or their confidence in the company. We pay attention to compensation issues but then also work on the real issues of management and leadership.

In addition, you need some kind of early warning system so that you always have a chance to get to people before they're out the door. In a company in difficulty, you can't presume that people are happy. So I've told my staff to sit down every day with everyone who reports to them and ask overtly how they're doing and if they're happy. That forces people to discuss their concerns. Most of them will be honest if you give them the opportunity, I've found.

Retaining people is only one facet of the challenge, though. You also have to keep them motivated, and smart people are not as motivated by money as they are by recognition. At Novell, we have something called the President's Award Program, an annual dinner at which we recognize individual accomplishments. We choose 20 of our top employees each year, and we invite them and their spouses to the dinner and give them plaques and stock option grants to recognize their accomplishments. These are simple gestures, but it's amazing what they do for people. Recognition like this makes it much harder for them to leave the company, and it keeps them much more engaged in their work.

Smart people also need to feel that they are part of the solution. Most companies make the mistake of putting their most creative people in places where their contributions are limited or where they're resented by others. If you put them in research, they're ghettoized. If you put them in product groups, no one likes them because they work differently than everyone else. If you put them in strategy jobs, they write wonderful documents that no one uses. And in a hierarchical company, you have some managers who are not as smart as the people who work for them. These managers act like colonels. They tell the smart person, "Take the hill!," and the smart person says, "But I've been thinking about this and—"And the colonel says, "No. Take the hill!" That kind of command and control does not work.

I've found that the best way to manage smart people is to let them self-organize so they can operate both inside and outside the management hierarchy. They report to a manager, but they also have the latitude to work on projects that interest them, regardless of whether they originate with their own manager. You tell them, "Look, I don't know how to solve this problem, so why don't you throw yourself at it and figure it out? Take the time and resources you need, and get it right." If they get frustrated and need to blow off steam, you invite them to talk to you directly—no go-betweens. At the same time, you discuss this new component of the person's work directly with his or her manager, and there are no reprisals when a smart person works outside a manager's jurisdiction. It's the complete opposite of the culture of fear.

To win the hearts and minds of your key employees, you have to communicate directly and physically with them. Videoconferencing, telephone, e-mail, and other tools don't cut it. Politicians use the handclasp, and so do the best industry leaders. Since I've been here, I've spent way too much time on our corporate jet. In the beginning, I routinely hit five cities a day. That lifestyle is grueling but utterly necessary. Eighty percent of winning is just showing up.

Rarely is a corporate culture embedded only in a company's people; it also tends to be embedded in the processes and systems of the company. Was that the case at Novell?

Yes, and it was a big problem. For example, we had to change our reward systems to make sure people stayed focused on our key objectives, and we had to do it in a very short time frame. When I first came to Novell, our salespeople knew that they were spending too much time selling through the channel and not enough selling directly to corporate customers. This practice led to huge inventory problems, which were very costly to us. So we set up quarterly objectives for direct selling, and we also introduced a new incentive program based on 25 points: if you earned at least 20 points, based on the fulfillment of your objectives, you got a 100% bonus at the end of the quarter. When people would come to me and complain—which they always did—I would ask, "What are your objectives for this quarter?" If they didn't know them, I'd call their bosses and make sure they knew that the objectives had to be clearly communicated down the line. Business as usual wasn't going to cut it.

Incidentally, not all systemic changes work. I've also learned that certain management techniques can actually make things worse when applied to a distressed culture. For example, I had always worked in companies with yearly and quarterly employee ranking systems, in which people were divided into three groups: overperforming, performing, and underperforming. So not long after I came here, we started a ranking program that graded on a curve: 45% into the overperforming group, 50% into the performing group, and 5% into the underperforming group. I didn't know—and certainly didn't intend it this way—that if you got the lowest grade, it was presumed that you were about to be fired. We started getting hate mail from people who argued that there was no way to rank people who worked as a team. The ranking system exacerbated the culture of fear and proved to be such a huge retention and motivation issue that we were forced to stop it after a year. In its place, we introduced a modified ranking program that better reflected overall employee performance.

Novell had a resurgence through 1999, so your efforts obviously paid off. But like many companies, particularly in the tech sector, it's now facing slackening demand, rapid technological change, and relentless competition. How do you keep the company buoyant through the ups and downs?

First of all, we take our cash position very, very seriously. I balance my personal checkbook to the penny every month, and we run the company in the same way—as if the cash were our personal money. My first rule of business is that when you run out of cash, you close the doors. Cash is the last bulwark. That's a simple rule, but it's one that executives too often forget. I was fortunate to learn it when Sun nearly ran out of cash in 1989. The CFO had to get a bank loan to keep the company afloat. So after we turned around Novell, I was careful to harvest assets. The goal was to collect cash, hoard it, manage it, and talk about it a lot.

Harvesting cash is particularly tricky for companies in distress, because that's when customers don't pay. We put in a set of objectives for the sales force based on cash collection, and we made it a point to get everybody thinking about saving money. That discipline is helping us in our current transition away from our packaged software and toward our new technology platform. Our sales are under pressure at the moment, but our balance sheet is in incredibly good shape. We have almost no inventory in the channel, more than $700 million in cash, strong positive cash flow from operations, and hundreds of millions in investments that, we hope, will generate more cash down the road. Our cash position allows us to go on as we are for a long, long time, but we expect revenues to grow again in 2002.

Reporters and stock analysts can be brutal on a CEO when a company goes through a downturn. What keeps you from getting discouraged? What gives you the perspective to keep leading Novell through difficult times?

Obviously, I have very good reasons for putting up with four years of turning around a business and struggling to make it successful in new markets. First, I actually like the network services space that Novell is in. We have an immense market opportunity in this area. As for those greatly exaggerated rumors of Novell's death, I try to take them in stride while working hard to educate the market about our real situation. You know, it's easy to sit on the outside and criticize the one who's making the decisions. Taking harsh criticism is part of any top executive's job.

Real leadership involves taking the heat and staying focused on the way to achieve the desired outcome. Look at Steve Case. In 1997, he decided to change AOL's pricing to a flat $21 per month. He shouldered unbelievable criticism for that. I remember being on a panel with him at the time, and he was introduced as the "most hated CEO in America." They played a busy signal as he walked on-stage. And he came out and said to the audience, "I'm sorry, I'm sorry. We're doing everything we can to get this right. But this is the decision we've made, and this strategy is the right one." Today, AOL is incredibly successful. No one doubts now that Steve was right, but everybody doubted him back then.

It helps that business leaders understand what their colleagues are experiencing and go out of their way to support one another. I'm fortunate to have lots of good relationships with the tech industry's leaders, many of whom I met when I was Sun's CTO. I recall a moment in May 2000 when Novell was forced to preannounce a bad quarter. That very afternoon, Steve Jobs called me and said, "I wanted you to know that I know what you're going through, but I respect what you're doing and I wish you the best of luck." The next call was from Dave Wetherell of CMGI, which has had ups and downs, too. He told me, "These things are hard, but you have to stick with your principles, stay with your focus, and you will win." I believe these people. In fact, I think people trust leaders who have toughed it out through crises more than those who've had easy sailing. In a way, the fact that Novell has gone through crises has made me a more credible leader. I'm still here, and I'm still fighting for the company.

One thing that helps me a lot—that keeps things in perspective—is flying. I'm a commercial pilot, and during my most recent training, I was doing a difficult maneuver called "circle to land." I was in a twin-engine plane, and I was wearing a kind of hood so that I couldn't see out the windows. The instructor had shut down half the instruments and one engine, and I had to fly by the few remaining indicators. Then, at 900 feet, the control tower switched the runway on me. I had to turn around within a mile and come in on the other runway. I did the maneuver successfully. When you fly a plane, as complicated as it is, there are only a few things that will kill you. You can run out of gas, fly too low, or go off course. In my world, it's a good metaphor. As long as we pay attention to the important things, we'll survive.

Back to the Network

AFTER NOVELL WAS FOUNDED IN 1983, its flagship product, NetWare, quickly became the de facto standard in operating system software for local area networks (LANs). But in the 1990s, two epochal events combined to undermine the company's leadership position. First, in late 1993, Microsoft entered the networking market with its Windows NT operating system. Second, the rise of the Internet created a powerful new standard for networking, rendering the old LAN architecture obsolete. Faced with an erosion of its core market, Novell launched an ill-fated diversification initiative, spending $1.5 billion to acquire packaged-software businesses such as WordPerfect Corporation to compete with Microsoft on the desktop. Thus distracted, Novell saw its grip on the networking market slip further, even as its new products failed to live up to the company's overly optimistic expectations.

Since taking over as chairman and CEO in 1997, Eric Schmidt has pulled Novell back to its networking roots while also guiding the company into the booming market for Internet-based products and services. At the core of Schmidt's strategy is a new product called eDirectory (founded on the Novell Directory Services platform). This software allows corporate IT departments to hold down the operational costs associated with locating and managing millions of "objects"—servers, PCs, notebooks, wireless devices, routers, application programs, files, and users—on ever expanding networks composed of complicated and diverse mini-networks. By developing and selling applications and services that take advantage of the eDirectory system and that operate across all computing platforms, Schmidt believes Novell can become a leader in the rapidly growing directory-services market.

The company's fortunes initially rebounded in 1999 with the successful launch of NetWare 5.0, its new, industrial-strength network operating system. And customers appear to be embracing the eDirectory system, opening up many new opportunities for the company. Indeed, the fastest growing segment of its business is applications such as ZEN-works and GroupWise, built to run on eDirectory.

But Novell is not out of the woods yet. In 2000, corporate technology spending began to slow, and Novell's revenues, like those of many high-tech companies, flattened. In March 2001, the company announced plans to acquire Cambridge Technology Partners, a global IT service provider, accelerating Novell's shift into services. As part of the acquisition, CTP CEO Jack Messman will succeed Schmidt as CEO of Novell. Schmidt will continue as the company's chairman and will also become its chief strategist.

Originally published in May 2001
Reprint R0105H

About the Contributors

TOM COPELAND is the director of the Corporate Finance Practice at Monitor Group, a consulting firm based in Cambridge, MA. He is the author of *Valuation: Measuring and Managing the Value of Companies*.

DIANE L. COUTU is a senior editor at HBR specializing in psychology and business.

BRONWYN FRYER is a senior editor at HBR.

ROSABETH MOSS KANTER is the Ernest L. Arbuckle Professor of Business Administration at Harvard Business School in Boston, specializing in strategy, innovation, and leadership for change.

ANTHONY J. MAYO is a lecturer and director of the Leadership Initiative at Harvard Business School in Boston.

NITIN NOHRIA is the Richard P. Chapman Professor of Business Administration at Harvard Business School in Boston.

MATTHEW S. OLSON is an executive director at the Corporate Executive Board.

DARRELL RIGBY is a director of Bain & Company in Boston.

ERIC SCHMIDT is Chairman and CEO of Google, Inc., and formerly the CEO of Novell, Inc.

DEREK VAN BEVER is the chief research officer at the Corporate Executive Board.

SETH VERRY is a senior director at the Corporate Executive Board.

CHRIS ZOOK is the author of *Unstoppable: Finding Hidden Assets to Renew the Core and Fuel Possible Growth*. He leads the Global Strategy Practice of Bain & Company.

Index